Be Prepared

PARTICIPANT'S GUIDE

TYNDALE HOUSE PUBLISHERS, INC.

Carol Stream, Illinois

Essentials of Parenting: Be Prepared
Participant's Guide

Copyright © 2011 by Focus on the Family
All rights reserved.

Focus on the Family and the accompanying logo and design are federally registered
trademarks of Focus on the Family, Colorado Springs, CO 80995.

A Focus on the Family book published by Tyndale House Publishers, Carol Stream,
Illinois 60188

TYNDALE is a registered trademark of Tyndale House Publishers, Inc. Tyndale's quill
logo is a trademark of Tyndale House Publishers, Inc.

All Scripture quotations, unless otherwise indicated, are taken from the *Holy Bible, New
International Version*®. NIV®. Copyright © 1973, 1978, 1984 by Biblica, Inc.™ Used
by permission of Zondervan. All rights reserved worldwide. (www.zondervan.com).

Cover design by Ron Kaufman
Cover photograph copyright © Fuse/Getty Images. All rights reserved.

Note: Portions of this book are adapted from *Lead Your Teen to a Lifelong Faith*, Joe
White and Jim Weidmann, general editors. ISBN: 1-58997-084-5. Copyright © 2005
by Focus on the Family.

ISBN: 978-1-58997-570-5

Printed in the United States of America
1 2 3 4 5 6 7 / 16 15 14 13 12 11

CONTENTS

QUICK START GUIDE FOR PARENTS

Whether you're studying in a group, as a couple, or individually, this book is for you. It's packed with discussion questions, advice, biblical input, and application activities.

But maybe all you'd like to do right now is watch the accompanying DVD and talk about it with your spouse—or think about it on your own. If so, go directly to the "Catching the Vision" section of each chapter. There you'll find the discussion questions you're looking for.

When you have more time, we encourage you to explore the other features in this book. We think you'll find them . . . essential!

WELCOME!

If there's anything you don't need, it's one more thing to do.

Unless, of course, that one thing might make the *other* things a whole lot easier.

We can't guarantee that this course will take all the challenge out of parenthood. It won't keep your kids from forgetting their lunch money, make them trade in their video games for art museum passes, or remind them to scoop the cat's litter box.

But it *will* help you understand why your parenting is so crucial, how to connect with your kids and encourage them to connect with their Creator, and how to enjoy the journey to the fullest. That's because you'll learn the essentials—what's vital to a healthy parent-child relationship, keys to protecting and training and affirming kids, and what God considers most important in bringing up boys and girls.

In other words, you'll discover how to be the mom or dad you really want to be.

That takes effort, but it doesn't take boredom or busywork. So we've designed this course to be provocative and practical. At its heart is an entertaining, down-to-earth video series featuring many of today's most popular parenting experts. And in your hands is the book that's going to make it all personal for you—the Participant's Guide.

In each chapter of this book, you'll find the following sections:

Finding Yourself. Take this survey to figure out where you stand on the subject at hand.

Catching the Vision. Use this section as you watch and think about the DVD.

Digging Deeper. This Bible study includes Scripture passages and thought-provoking questions.

Making It Work. Practice makes perfect, so here's your chance to begin applying principles from the DVD to your own family.

Bringing It Home. To wrap up, you'll find specific, encouraging advice you can use this week.

Whether you're using this book as part of a group or on your own, taking a few minutes to read and complete each chapter will bring the messages of the DVD home.

And isn't that exactly where you need it most?

Note: Many issues addressed in this series are difficult ones. Some parents may need to address them in greater detail and depth. The DVD presentations and this guide are intended as general advice only, and not to replace clinical counseling, medical treatment, legal counsel, or pastoral guidance.

Focus on the Family maintains a referral network of Christian counselors. For information, call 1-800-A-FAMILY and ask for the counseling department. You can also find plenty of parenting advice and encouragement at www.focusonthefamily.com.

Chapter 1

PROTECT OR PREPARE?

Just a few days ago I talked with a mom I'll call Sarah. She *wants* to be responsible for the safety of her 16-year-old son, Luke. Why? Because then things will turn out the way she wants them to—or so her illusion goes.

She wants God to be the One who looks out for Luke's best interests—as long as He does it according to her specifications. In Sarah's theology, God is sovereign and that's "okay" with her—almost as if God needs her permission. In everyday life, though, *she* wants that position of sovereign control—at least when it comes to her son.

Sarah called me because her illusion of control had just been shattered. So had her illusion that her prayers could make God do as she wished—namely, keep Luke "safe." She wanted her illusions back. She wanted control over Luke's life.

As we talked, I pressed Sarah with questions:

"Who's the one really in charge of Luke—you or God?"

"Is God really sovereign all the time, or only on Sundays?"

"Why did God allow Adam and Eve to eat from the forbidden tree? Why didn't He stop them?"

"If God really is in charge, why are you trying to tell Him how best to handle things with Luke? Isn't that sort of playing God, in effect making God your genie in a bottle and telling Him how to run the world of 'Luke'?"

Sarah wrestled with my questions. But when she replied, it was like this: "Luke is my son, and I don't want him to get hurt. I want to be sure he stays safe [by my criteria]."

Notice the pronouns in Sarah's thinking?

Losing control—even the perception of control—of your child and what may befall him or her can be scary. Yet it's also freeing. And it's better for you . . . and for him or her.

—Tim Sanford, Licensed Professional Counselor[1]

Identifying Your Needs

Here's a survey; please take a few minutes to fill it out.

1. If you could, you'd like to shelter your child from
   ___ wind, rain, snow, sleet, and fungal infections.
   ___ TV, movies, skimpy bathing suits, and midnight bowling.
   ___ taxes.
   ___ other _____

2. So far, you've been able to control your child's environment
   ___ by moving to a reinforced concrete bunker in an undisclosed location.
   ___ through manipulation and threats.
   ___ in your dreams.
   ___ other _____

3. Knowing the difference between control and influence is
   ___ unimportant.
   ___ a key to your relationship with your child.
   ___ a sneaky way to control your kids.
   ___ other _____

4. If you could, you'd like to equip your child to
   ___ stand up to temptation and false religions.
   ___ adapt to today's world.
   ___ grow up to be just like you.
   ___ other _____

5. So far, you've been able to equip your child to
   ___ speak Latin and complete law school 10 years early.
   ___ counsel troubled peers and evangelize unreached people groups.
   ___ eat a Ding Dong without smearing chocolate all over her face.
   ___ other _____

6. If God created every child with a free will,
   ___ your daughter may not want to be sheltered or controlled.
   ___ your efforts to make your son turn out "right" may be doomed.
   ___ life is probably not worth living.
   ___ other _____

CATCHING THE VISION

Watching and Discussing the DVD

The world can be a dangerous place. Some parents respond by sticking their heads in the sand. Others lock kids in their rooms, more or less, to keep the cultural wolves at bay.

In this DVD segment, Dr. Bob Barnes, executive director of Sheridan House Family Ministries, has a better idea. Author of several books including *Ready for Responsibility: How to Equip Your Children for Work and Marriage* (Zondervan, 1996), Dr. Barnes suggests that denial and overprotection aren't the answer. Our kids need us to *equip* them for the worlds of today and tomorrow.

Joining Bob is Dr. Juli Slattery, family psychologist and broadcast host for Focus on the Family; her books include *No More Headaches* (Focus on the Family/Tyndale, 2009) and *Guilt-Free Motherhood* (HCI, 2004).

As Bob and Juli can attest, equipping takes time. But so do all the forms of what might well be called . . . discipleship.

After viewing the DVD, use questions like these to help you think through what you saw and heard.

1. Which of the following statements might be made by a parent who's in denial about the world's dangers? Which might be made by a parent who's too sheltering? Which come closest to statements you might make?
   - "Racy pictures are nothing new; boys were looking at them long before the Internet was invented."
   - "I don't care if you're 'old enough' for PG-13. If it's not something our whole family can watch, you're not watching it, either."
   - "You can learn about missions right here; you don't have to go to some Third World country that's full of disease."
   - "Yeah, you can go to the sleepover. I'm sure the parents are okay if their kids go to your school."
   - "I'd like you to stop going out with him. His church doesn't do baptism the same way we do."

2. Which of the following scriptures do you think would be most helpful to a parent who's trying to find a balance between sheltering and equipping? Why?
   - John 17
   - 2 Timothy 3:16-17
   - 2 Timothy 1:7

3. If you could ask Dr. Bob Barnes one question, what would it be? If he watched you parent your child for a week, what do you think he might say about your approach to sheltering and equipping? Why?

4. How equipped (0 percent to 100 percent) would you say your child is to do each of the following? Based on what you saw in the DVD presentation, what would you like to do about that?
   - Tell a friend at least one good reason to believe that God exists.
   - Resist the temptation to cheat on a test.
   - Use a credit card wisely.
   - Respond lovingly but firmly to a person who uses a racial slur.

5. How is equipping a child a form of discipleship? Who's the disciple? Whose disciple is he or she? What if the disciple doesn't want to cooperate?

Bible Study

> *David said to Saul, "Let no one lose heart on account of this Philistine; your servant will go and fight him."*
>
> *Saul replied, "You are not able to go out against this Philistine and fight him; you are only a boy, and he has been a fighting man from his youth."*
>
> *But David said to Saul, ". . . The* LORD *who delivered me from the paw of the lion and the paw of the bear will deliver me from the hand of this Philistine."*
>
> *Saul said to David, "Go, and the* LORD *be with you."*
>
> *Then Saul dressed David in his own tunic. He put a coat of armor on him and a bronze helmet on his head. David fastened on his sword over the tunic and tried walking around, because he was not used to them.*

"I cannot go in these," he said to Saul, "because I am not used to them." So he took them off. Then he took his staff in his hand, chose five smooth stones from the stream, put them in the pouch of his shepherd's bag and, with his sling in his hand, approached the Philistine. (1 Samuel 17:32-34, 37-40)

1. How did Saul try to shelter David? How did he try to equip him? Why didn't those approaches work? Based on this experience, what might David tell parents about protecting and preparing children?

"But if serving the LORD seems undesirable to you, then choose for yourselves this day whom you will serve, whether the gods your forefathers served beyond the River, or the gods of the Amorites, in whose land you are living. But as for me and my household, we will serve the LORD." (Joshua 24:15)

2. When do you think was the last time your child faced the choice of whether to serve God or not? What happened? When do you think the next time might be? How will you encourage your child to choose wisely—without trying to control him or her?

When the woman saw that the fruit of the tree was good for food and pleasing to the eye, and also desirable for gaining wisdom, she took some and ate it. She also gave some to her husband, who was with her, and he ate it. Then the eyes of both of them were opened, and they realized they were naked; so they sewed fig leaves together and made coverings for themselves.

Then the man and his wife heard the sound of the LORD God as he was walking in the garden in the cool of the day, and they hid from the LORD God among the trees of the garden. But the LORD God called to the man, "Where are you?"

> *He answered, "I heard you in the garden, and I was afraid because I*
> *was naked; so I hid."*
> *And he said, "Who told you that you were naked? Have you eaten*
> *from the tree that I commanded you not to eat from?"*
> *The man said, "The woman you put here with me—she gave me*
> *some fruit from the tree, and I ate it."*
> *Then the LORD God said to the woman, "What is this you have done?"*
> *The woman said, "The serpent deceived me, and I ate." (Genesis*
> *3:6-13)*

3. Why didn't God protect His children, Adam and Eve, from making the wrong choice in the Garden of Eden? What was the result? What might Adam and Eve tell parents about sheltering and protecting children?

> *Now Eli, who was very old, heard about everything his sons were*
> *doing to all Israel and how they slept with the women who served at the*
> *entrance to the Tent of Meeting. So he said to them, "Why do you do such*
> *things? I hear from all the people about these wicked deeds of yours. No,*
> *my sons; it is not a good report that I hear spreading among the LORD's*
> *people. If a man sins against another man, God may mediate for him;*
> *but if a man sins against the LORD, who will intercede for him?" His*
> *sons, however, did not listen to their father's rebuke, for it was the LORD's*
> *will to put them to death.*
> *And the boy Samuel continued to grow in stature and in favor with*
> *the LORD and with men. (1 Samuel 2:22-26)*

4. What do you think Eli might tell parents about trying to make their kids turn out right? In the end, was he able to shelter his sons from the consequences of their actions? Was he able to equip Samuel? What does that tell you about the role of parents in their children's lives?

Applying the Principles

How much control do you really have over your child's behavior? For each of the following "controls," rate the percentage you have over each— and the percentage your child has.

STEERING CLEAR OF DRUG USE

% of control you have _____

% of control your child has _____

WORKING FASTER ON HOMEWORK

% of control you have _____

% of control your child has _____

PUTTING A STOP TO HARMFUL FRIENDSHIPS

% of control you have _____

% of control your child has _____

HAVING A BIBLICAL WORLDVIEW

% of control you have _____

% of control your child has _____

ENTERTAINMENT CHOICES

% of control you have _____

% of control your child has _____

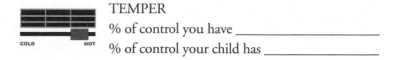

TEMPER

% of control you have _____

% of control your child has _____

Have you ever tried to "grab the wheel" of your child's life, or "stomp on the brake"? If so, what happened?

How might your child's age and maturity affect your answers?

What percentages do you think your child would assign to each "control"?

Now choose one of the controls that you can start to "let up on" this week. What could be your first step in that process?

Insight for Your Week

Let's consider the Garden of Eden again. In this perfect place with perfect children and a perfect parent, there was a rule.

It was, "You must not eat from the tree of the knowledge of good and evil" (Genesis 2:17). It wasn't, "You *shouldn't* eat of that tree," or "Stay away from dangerous fruit." It was a simple, clear command not to eat from a specific tree.

Why was there a rule in the Garden? The answer lies in the two reasons for any rule:

1. To keep safety in.
2. To keep chaos (un-safety) out.

That's as complicated as it gets. That's it.

Since you probably don't have a dictionary with you, let me review what safety and chaos mean.

Safety is being protected from damage or danger—physical, emotional, and spiritual.

The "damage" part of that definition is important. There are two kinds of hurt—the kind that causes actual damage and the kind that doesn't. Parents often get them mixed up.

In our attempt to be responsible parents, we sometimes think our job is to protect our children from *all* pain—both kinds. But the second kind of pain is part of living and growing up. It's the first kind, the type that produces damage, that we're striving to protect our children from.

Chaos is a place or circumstance of confusion or disorder. Safety is compromised here, and the "damage" kind of pain is likely to happen.

With those definitions behind us, let's look at the rule in Genesis. Why did God put that tree off-limits? Because "you will surely die" (2:17). That's definitely a safety issue. It's all about damage.

Rules aren't for modifying behavior, instilling values, or changing attitudes. Here's where parents often go astray, writing regulations that attempt to do exactly these things.

It doesn't work. If you want to influence behavior or instill values or work on attitudes, you'll model, mentor, teach, and pray—over and over again.

If you could have only *five* household rules, what would they be?

Make a written list. Be sure your rules are specific, clear, and enforceable. Cover everything you deem important for safety. But you can have only five.

And no rule is allowed to have 65 sub-rules!

I gave this assignment to Gary and Rita when I was helping them work with their 16-year-old son. Rita came back a week later with nine typewritten pages. There were only five numbered rules, per my instructions, but each rule had multiple sub-rules.

Rita was trying to pack as much into those five regulations as she could. Her real motive was to control her son Jared's every behavior and attitude.

I sent Rita and Gary home to try again, asking them to create five simple, clear rules. By the next appointment, Rita had pared her nine pages down to three. "It was the best I could do," she said.

Still, she had too many sneaky addendums to each rule. After talking about the reason for rules and Rita's reasons for her three pages, I sent the couple home yet again with the same assignment.

By the end of the third session, Rita and Gary finally understood. They wrestled with their motives for controlling Jared. They came to see that they couldn't control him, that it wasn't their job, and that they could make and enforce rules to keep safety in and chaos out.

What will your five rules be? Separate them from principles you choose to teach. Also, make a list of important items that fall into the "suggestions" category.

There's nothing magical or "psychological" about the number five. The purpose is to help you think small—as well as simply, clearly, and specifically. You may end up with a few more than five rules, and that's fine. Just let me emphasize the word "few." Make sure these rules are clear in your own mind so that you can state them plainly to your children.

—Tim Sanford, Licensed Professional Counselor[2]

Chapter 2

THE FACTS OF LIFE AND OTHER FEARS

For decades, movies and sitcoms have presented a caricature of the sweaty-palmed, birds-and-bees conversation in which Dad stammers through a convoluted description of sex to a preadolescent child—who, it turns out, knows all of the details already. The humor arises from the tension most parents feel about discussing sex with their kids. ("What if we tell him too much?" "Will this rob him of his innocence?" "What if he starts asking about what we do?")

What isn't so funny is the reality that too many children learn about sex from everyone but their parents. Playground slang and obscenity, a distorted description of intercourse from the tough kid up the street, or worst of all, a look at some pornographic material on cable TV or the Internet often provides a child's first jarring glimpse of sex. What should be seen as the most beautiful, meaningful, and private communication between a married couple becomes a freak-show curiosity.

Efforts by public schools to correct misinformation from the street and lack of information from home often leave out a critical ingredient: the moral framework within which the facts about reproduction should be presented. Without an ethical context, sex education becomes little more than basic training in anatomy, physiology, infectious diseases, and contraception.

Many churches have made laudable efforts to teach biblical principles of sexuality to their youth groups. But these important concepts are not always accompanied by accurate medical information or refusal skills. Furthermore, youth-group presentations usually begin late in the game (i.e., during the teen years) and rarely involve an ongoing dialogue about this subject.

The best place for a child to learn about sexuality is at home from those who care most about him. Anyone can teach the basic facts about reproduction in an hour or two (or they can be read in any of several reference books), but you are in the best position to put this information in the proper context and give it the right perspective over a period of years.

—Paul C. Reisser, M.D.[3]

Identifying Your Needs

Here's a questionnaire to get you thinking about your opinions on parenting and sexuality.

1. The wisest advice you ever heard on the subject of teaching kids about sex was

    ____ "Train a child in the way he should go, and when he is old he will not turn from it" (Proverbs 22:6).

    ____ "Listen, my son, to your father's instruction and do not forsake your mother's teaching" (Proverbs 1:8).

    ____ "Just give 'em a book and run out of the room."

    ____ other _____

2. When it comes to giving children a healthy view of sexuality, the problem with most parents is

____ not knowing what to say.

____ not knowing when to say it.

____ not knowing where to hide until it's all over.

____ other _____

3. Our culture's idea of sex education is

    ____ letting kids listen to songs about infidelity, lust, prostitution, and assault.

    ____ watching old black-and-white films about fifth graders who don't want to get "cooties."

    ____ spring break.

    ____ other _____

4. Raising kids who won't have premarital sex is harder than it used to be because

    ____ the media don't support traditional values anymore.

    ____ parents feel guilty about not having "waited" themselves.

    ____ the Teletubbies ruined everything.

    ____ other _____

5. Young people shouldn't begin dating until

    ____ they understand what they're looking for in a marriage partner.

    ____ the courtship approach doesn't work out.

    ____ *Disney on Ice* begins to lose its appeal.

    ____ other _____

6. If you could make our culture's approach to sexuality more parent-friendly, you would

    ____ ban Internet porn.

    ____ ban divorce.

    ____ ban hormones.

    ____ other _____

Watching and Discussing the DVD

When it comes to teaching kids about sex, how do parents get past the infamous awkwardness? They don't. But according to Dannah Gresh and Ron Luce, they need to tackle the task anyway.

Dannah is a mother-daughter relationship coach and popular speaker whose books include *Lies Young Women Believe* (Moody, 2008), co-authored with Nancy Leigh DeMoss. In this DVD segment, she talks about the question of what children need to know about sexuality and when, as well as issues like modesty, crushes, boyfriends, and girlfriends. Ron Luce is co-founder and president of Teen Mania Ministries and author of several books including *Re-Create: Building a Culture in Your Home Stronger Than the Culture Deceiving Your Kids* (Regal, 2008).

How can you encourage your kids to wait for marriage when it seems everyone is "watching it, wearing it, and doing it"? This session builds confidence in parents by providing specific, down-to-earth advice based on real-world experience.

After viewing the DVD, use questions like these to help you think through what you saw and heard.

1. If your child asked you the following questions at age five, what would be the essence of your answers? What if your child were eleven? What principles are you following in deciding what your answers would be?
   - "Where do babies come from?"
   - "How are boys and girls different?"
   - "Why are those people on TV taking their clothes off?"

2. How could you admit to your child that you feel awkward talking about sex—without letting it stop you? Which of the following might work for you?

- "I hate doing this, so let's get it over with."
- "I don't know what I'm talking about, so bear with me."
- "I know there are easier things to discuss, but it's really important that we do."
- other _____

3. What do you like best about Dannah Gresh's approach to this topic? Which of the following might you be able to use this week? How?
    - a phrase she mentioned _____
    - her honesty and transparency
    - her advice about crushes
    - her advice about modesty
    - other _____

4. What's an example you've seen of each of the following? How did you respond? Would you recommend your response to the rest of the group? Why or why not?
    - a time your child heard something about sex that you needed to put in context
    - a time when you wished you'd addressed earlier an issue like how to treat the opposite sex, dating expectations, or provocative clothing
    - a time when your child made a wise choice concerning sexuality or dating

5. What would you like to tell your child about the following? If it's hard for you to do that, how can our group pray for your efforts?
    - abstinence
    - Bratz and Barbie dolls
    - the permanence of marriage
    - protecting oneself from sexual predators
    - choosing the right people to date
    - other _____

Bible Study

> *Don't let anyone look down on you because you are young, but set an*
> *example for the believers in speech, in life, in love, in faith and in purity.*
> *(1 Timothy 4:12)*

1. When it comes to abstaining from sex outside of marriage, how do some adults "look down on" young people? Are kids today expected to set an example in "purity"? Why or why not?

2. How might taking this verse seriously affect the following?
   a. church youth groups
   b. school sex education classes
   c. the way you talk to your child about sexuality

> *Now to the unmarried and the widows I say: It is good for them*
> *to stay unmarried, as I am. But if they cannot control themselves,*
> *they should marry, for it is better to marry than to burn with passion.*
> *(1 Corinthians 7:8-9)*

3. Would you say that the apostle Paul was more enthused or less enthused about marriage than most young people in our culture are today? If you were talking with your child about dating and ran into this passage, how would you explain it?

> *A woman is bound to her husband as long as he lives. But if her husband dies, she is free to marry anyone she wishes, but he must belong to the Lord. (1 Corinthians 7:39)*

4. Why do you think Paul gave this advice? If you wanted to convince your child that Christians should marry only Christians, how would you do it?

> For although they knew God, they neither glorified him as God nor gave thanks to him, but their thinking became futile and their foolish hearts were darkened. Although they claimed to be wise, they became fools and exchanged the glory of the immortal God for images made to look like mortal man and birds and animals and reptiles.
>
> Therefore God gave them over in the sinful desires of their hearts to sexual impurity for the degrading of their bodies with one another. They exchanged the truth of God for a lie, and worshiped and served created things rather than the Creator—who is forever praised. Amen. . . .
>
> You, therefore, have no excuse, you who pass judgment on someone else, for at whatever point you judge the other, you are condemning yourself, because you who pass judgment do the same things. (Romans 1:21-25; 2:1)

5. What parts of this passage do you think describe society and the church today? If this description fits today, how can parents hope to teach their children healthy attitudes about sexuality?

> How can a young man keep his way pure? By living according to your word. I seek you with all my heart; do not let me stray from your commands. I have hidden your word in my heart that I might not sin against you. (Psalm 119:9-11)

6. How could you help your child adopt this strategy where sex is concerned? What evidence could you give that it's important? What evidence could you give that it works?

Applying the Principles

What do you think of the following parenting ideas? Would you follow them? Why or why not?

1. "It's better to let your teenager make out with his girlfriend in his room than to force them to fool around in the backseat of a car."
   ___ I would follow this advice.
   ___ This part of the advice is true: _____
   ___ This part of the advice is false: _____
   ___ This advice has no value whatsoever.

2. "Your son may be looking at porn on the Internet, but it's not worth harming your relationship by embarrassing him with a confrontation about it."
   ___ I would follow this advice.
   ___ This part of the advice is true: _____
   ___ This part of the advice is false: _____
   ___ This advice has no value whatsoever.

3. "Tell your preteen that she should wait until she's ready to have sex."
   ___ I would follow this advice.
   ___ This part of the advice is true: _____
   ___ This part of the advice is false: _____
   ___ This advice has no value whatsoever.

4. "Since kids shouldn't get married until they have jobs or finish college, they shouldn't date until then, either."
   ___ I would follow this advice.

____ This part of the advice is true: _____

____ This part of the advice is false: _____

____ This advice has no value whatsoever.

5. "If your teen is sexually active, help him or her to obtain contraception as soon as possible."

____ I would follow this advice.

____ This part of the advice is true: _____

____ This part of the advice is false: _____

____ This advice has no value whatsoever.

6. "If your teen announces that he or she is gay, accept it and celebrate it."

____ I would follow this advice.

____ This part of the advice is true: _____

____ This part of the advice is false: _____

____ This advice has no value whatsoever.

7. "Unless you're an expert, just give your child a book about sexuality and let him or her read it."

____ I would follow this advice.

____ This part of the advice is true: _____

____ This part of the advice is false: _____

____ This advice has no value whatsoever.

8. "Children don't want to know about sexuality until they reach puberty, so don't bring it up."

____ I would follow this advice.

____ This part of the advice is true: _____

____ This part of the advice is false: _____

____ This advice has no value whatsoever.

9. "Christians shouldn't marry non-Christians, so they shouldn't date them, either."

___ I would follow this advice.

___ This part of the advice is true: _____

___ This part of the advice is false: _____

___ This advice has no value whatsoever.

10. "Keep your bedroom door locked, because if your child discovers you and your spouse having a sexual encounter, your child will be emotionally scarred for life."

___ I would follow this advice.

___ This part of the advice is true: _____

___ This part of the advice is false: _____

___ This advice has no value whatsoever.

BRINGING IT HOME

Insight for Your Week

What can parents do to reduce the risk of premarital adolescent sex? Plenty.

Be aware of the specific risk factors for teen sex:

- Alcohol and drug use.
- A steady boyfriend or girlfriend.
- Little parental monitoring.
- A parental belief that adolescent sex is appropriate.
- A parental belief that adolescent sex is inevitable.
- Low grade point average/low attachment to school.
- A history of physical or sexual abuse.
- Frequent family relocations.
- Only one parent in the household.

The latter does not mean that adolescent sex is inevitable in single-parent families. But it does place an additional responsibility on single parents to send their teenagers clear and consistent messages about sexuality. And it is one more reason for single parents to enlist as much support as they can.

Understand the specific factors that lower the risk for teen sex:

- Religious commitment.
- Educational accomplishment/commitment to school.
- Friends who have a similar commitment to abstinence.
- Presence of both parents in the home, especially the biological father.
- Parental and community values that support and clearly promote sexual abstinence until marriage.
- Having a host of other interesting activities and passions.

Be a role model for the kinds of relationships you want your kids to develop with members of the opposite sex.

Do your best to give your teen(s) a strong, positive sense of identity.

Create a special occasion to talk about abstaining from sex until marriage.

If your adolescent has already had sexual experiences, make it clear that it is never too late to make a commitment to reserve sex for marriage.

Continue sending healthy messages about sexuality throughout your son's or daughter's adolescent years.

Talk about healthy and unhealthy relationships, and train your adolescent to avoid situations that increase the likelihood of a sexual incident.

Set up your expectations and ground rules about dating in advance—well before your teenager asks if he or she can go out with someone.

Talk candidly to your daughter(s) about the unpleasant topic of date rape and how best to avoid it.

Talk explicitly to your son(s) about respect for members of the opposite sex and about sexual responsibility.

Share guidelines like these for teenagers on dates and other occasions:

- Establish clear and unequivocal respect for your body, your life, and your future. Decide *before* the conversation, *before* the date, *before* the relationship gets more serious that physical intimacy is reserved for your wedding night.
- Respecting yourself (and the person you're with) means setting your own limits for physical contact. Stick to them, and be ready to defend them if necessary.
- Physical contact—even something as simple as holding hands—may be interpreted in ways you don't intend. What to you means "I like you" or "I think you're okay" might be received as "I'm madly in love with you" or "I want to go further."
- Remember that the events that lead to sex are progressive. Think of a car gaining momentum as it coasts down a steep hill. Once a given level of intimacy has been reached, it is very difficult to back up to a more conservative one. It is also more difficult to defend a boundary in the heat of the moment.
- You are much better off setting very conservative limits for expressing affection (holding hands and perhaps a brief embrace or kiss) and progressing slowly, both emotionally and physically, in a relationship. This isn't old-fashioned but smart and realistic.
- If you're not sure whether what you're doing physically is appropriate, ask yourself if you would be comfortable doing it in front of either set of parents, your pastor, or your future spouse. Remember that the person you are with now will probably not be the person you will marry. Would you feel comfortable having that person watch what you're doing?
- If resisting physical intimacy is becoming more difficult, don't tempt fate. Stay away from situations where the two of you are alone together. Deliberately plan to be around other people or in places where nothing can happen. Don't lie down on the sofa together to watch a video, and don't watch movies or videos with

overt sexual content. Don't banter sexually provocative comments back and forth on the assumption that talk is safer than sex. Remember that your most important sexual organ is your mind, and where it goes your body will follow.

—Paul C. Reisser, M.D.[4]

Chapter 3

PREVENTING DISORDERS OF SELF-WORTH

Whether they are National Merit Scholars or total nonconformists (or both), adolescents are fervently searching for a clear sense of identity. Whatever the guise or getup, the questions they continually ask boil down to these: *Who cares about me?* and *What can I do that has any significance?*

If the answers are "my God, my family, and my close friends" and "impact the world in a positive way," your main task—and it usually will be a pleasant one—will be serving as cheerleader and sounding board as your son or daughter finds the best track on which to run.

If the answers are "my friends (and hardly anyone else)" and "have fun (and hardly anything else)," the ultimate outcome could be more un-predictable. Most adolescents with this mind-set eventually grow up and find a productive niche, while some stay in this shallow, meandering rut well into adulthood. Some also drift into drug use or sexual activity in their search for the next diversion—and ultimately pay dearly for it.

For the teenager whose answers are "no one" and "nothing," if differ-ent answers are nowhere on the horizon, the consequences may be more serious: depression, acting out, even suicidal behavior.

Obviously, it is important that your child enter adolescence with some clear and positive answers to the questions of caring and signifi-cance. During the coming seasons, he will probably ask them often and in many different ways—some of which may catch you way off guard.

Even if he has lost his bearings or abandoned common sense, you will still need to communicate that your love and his significance are unshakable. As in earlier years of childhood, you will need to enforce limits and help him make some course corrections until he is on his own. But he must always know that your fundamental love for him will never change, regardless of grades, clothes, a messy room, dented fenders, or more serious issues.

—Paul C. Reisser, M.D.[5]

Identifying Your Needs

Take a couple of minutes to fill out the following survey.

1. When you were a child, how often did your parents say something encouraging to you?
    a. at least once a day
    b. once a week, unless you hadn't taken a shower recently
    c. on your birthday, instead of giving you a present
    d. other _____

2. The difference between flattering your child and praising him is
    a. the degree of your sincerity
    b. your motivation
    c. not worth mentioning, since you don't plan to do either
    d. other _____

3. When is it hardest to encourage your child?
    a. when she's feeling guilty about a bad habit
    b. when she's feeling depressed about a broken dream

c. when she's strangling you with one hand and picking your pocket with the other

d. other _____

4. When you hear the term "self-esteem," what do you think of?
   a. believing that you're worth something
   b. believing that you're worth nothing
   c. believing you should get a trophy every time you blow your nose
   d. other _____

5. How have you encouraged your child to have a good self-image?
   a. by banning Barbie dolls in your home
   b. by banning action figures in your home
   c. by banning mirrors in your home
   d. other _____

6. Which of the following statements would best build your child's self-worth?
   a. "God don't make no junk."
   b. "You look like a million bucks."
   c. "You're almost as cool as I am."
   d. other _____

CATCHING THE VISION

Watching and Discussing the DVD

How much is your child worth? Tragically, many kids these days would mark their "price tags" much too low. Despite all the talk of self-esteem, a disturbing number of young people who don't value themselves fall prey to depression, eating disorders, and self-mutilation.

This session's DVD segment features two experts on problems of self-worth. Dr. Dena Cabrera is a psychologist at Remuda Ranch Programs for Eating and Anxiety Disorders. Jerusha Clark is a writer and speaker who's authored or co-authored at least 10 books—including *Every Thought Captive* (Th1nk Books, 2006) and *Inside a Cutter's Mind* (Nav-Press, 2007).

What should parents do about weight problems and anorexia? How can they convince a daughter that she's truly beautiful? What if a son is cutting himself or practicing another form of self-destruction? The answers aren't always simple, but they begin with the principles presented in this session.

After viewing the DVD, use questions like these to help you think through what you saw and heard.

1. Which of the following thoughts might lead parents to think this video doesn't apply to them? How might Dr. Dena Cabrera and Jerusha Clark respond?
   - *My child is a boy, not a girl.*
   - *My child has lots of friends.*
   - *My child is a Christian.*
   - *My child is a success in school.*
   - *My child is talented and good-looking.*
   - *My child doesn't talk about feeling inferior.*

2. What messages about body image would your child get from watching the following? What messages about body image may he or she have gotten from watching you?
   - *The Biggest Loser*
   - Oprah Winfrey
   - the Miss Universe pageant
   - *America's Next Top Model*

3. If Jerusha and Dena came to your home, which of the following changes in your routine might they recommend? Which would you accept? Which would you resist? Why?
   - Don't make so many comments about your child's appearance, your appearance, or the appearance of others.
   - Serve healthier meals and make healthier snacks available.
   - If you're a dad and have a daughter, talk more about how valuable she is to you.
   - Show your child better ways to deal with stress.
   - Pray more, and start writing in a journal.

4. "Cutting" is often an effort to do one or more of the following. How might you help your child to accomplish the same goals without the self-destructive behavior?
   - making a cry for help or attention
   - relieving guilt
   - making up for not being "good enough"
   - being part of a social trend
   - feeling better through the release of endorphins

5. If you suspected that one of your child's friends had an eating disorder or a "cutting" habit, which of the following would you do? Why?
   - call the police
   - tell the parents
   - recommend a counselor
   - talk to the child who has the problem
   - let your child take care of it
   - pray
   - nothing
   - other _____

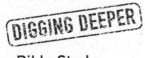

Bible Study

> *Therefore encourage one another and build each other up, just as in fact you are doing. (1 Thessalonians 5:11)*

1. How is encouraging your child like encouraging an adult acquaintance at church? How is it different?

   In which of the following areas does your child need to be "built up": (a) concern about his or her appearance, (b) confidence in making friends, (c) belief that God loves him or her, (d) hope for his or her future, or (e) something else?

   > *But encourage one another daily, as long as it is called Today, so that none of you may be hardened by sin's deceitfulness. (Hebrews 3:13)*

2. On average, how many times per day do you say or write something encouraging to your child? Are you satisfied with that? Do you think he or she is?

   > *And we urge you, brothers, warn those who are idle, encourage the timid, help the weak, be patient with everyone. (1 Thessalonians 5:14)*

3. When it comes to spiritual growth, does your child tend to be idle, timid, or weak? According to this verse, does he or she most need warnings, encouragement, or help?

   In which of these areas does your child tend to be most timid: (a) sharing her faith, (b) dreaming big dreams, (c) asking God for things, (d) getting involved with others at church, or (e) standing up to peer pressure?

Based on your previous answer, what do you most need to encourage your child to be or do?

Are not two sparrows sold for a penny? Yet not one of them will fall to the ground apart from the will of your Father. And even the very hairs of your head are all numbered. So don't be afraid; you are worth more than many sparrows. (Matthew 10:29-31)

4. Would this passage help to convince your child of his or her God-given value? If your child might find the sparrow analogy hard to relate to, what comparison could you suggest?

Like one who takes away a garment on a cold day, or like vinegar poured on soda, is one who sings songs to a heavy heart. (Proverbs 25:20)

5. When might a parent's "cheerleading" be annoying to a child? How can you tell when to back off and let your child be "heavy-hearted" for a while?

Applying the Principles

1. Have you noticed any of the following symptoms of low self-worth in your child?
    a. depression
    b. cutting
    c. an eating disorder
    d. negative comments about himself or herself
    e. other _____

2. If you've noticed such symptoms, which of the following "threat levels" would you assign to your situation?

RED: SEVERE

Severe Risk of Physical or Emotional Danger for Your Child

ORANGE: HIGH

High Risk of Physical or Emotional Danger for Your Child

YELLOW: ELEVATED

Elevated Risk of Physical or Emotional Danger for Your Child

BLUE: GUARDED

General Risk of Physical or Emotional Danger for Your Child

GREEN: LOW

Low Risk of Physical or Emotional Danger for Your Child

---

3. Based on your answer to the previous question, which of the following actions do you need to take this week?
   a. make an appointment with a counselor
   b. make an appointment with a pediatrician or other physician
   c. call the police
   d. ask friends to pray for you and your child
   e. have a talk with your child

f. give your child a hug

g. other _____

4. In which of the following ways would you prefer to encourage your child this week? Choose three; write a 1, 2, or 3 in the blank to indicate the order in which you plan to do them.

____ face-to-face conversation

____ phone conversation

____ e-mail

____ letter

____ hug

____ gift

____ special meal

____ eye contact

____ other _____

5. It's been said that parents should make five (or even ten) positive comments for every negative remark they make to their children. Can you come up with that many "cheers" for your child? To help you along, here are some possibilities. Mark your ten favorites; then add five of your own.

____ You are so thoughtful!

____ This is a tremendous improvement!

____ Good for you!

____ You are such a joy to us!

____ I never did that well when I was your age!

____ You handled that beautifully!

____ That's incredible!

____ You're really special to me—and getting more special every day!

____ I really enjoy being with you!

____ What a super effort!

___ The guy (girl) who marries you will be so lucky!

___ Your mom and I are so grateful to be your parents!

___ I really enjoy your smile!

___ That's fabulous!

___ There you go! That's it!

___ You're so helpful! Thank you!

___ You're going to make it!

___ I wish I could have done it that well!

___ I'm impressed!

___ I know you worked very hard on that. Wonderful job!

___ I love to hear your laugh!

___ I really like that!

___ I believe in you!

___ Excellent! That's the way to do it.

___ I love you![6]

other _____

other _____

other _____

other _____

other _____

other _____

Insight for Your Week

While excessive body fat is a continuing physical and emotional problem for millions of children and adolescents, powerful cultural forces provoke behaviors that pose even more serious threats to the young. We are saturated night and day with powerful images of beautiful, shapely, impossibly sleek women or buff, tight-muscled masculinity. This leads many, especially prepubertal and adolescent girls, into dangerous thinking: *If only I could look like* that, *my problems would be over.* Often this fantasy fuels a deeply felt desire for physical perfection that collides rudely with the imperfect appearance of a very real body seen in the mirror.

The conflict can lead not only to erratic eating habits and dieting, which are not without some risks, but also to the more severely disordered eating patterns known as *bulimia* and *anorexia nervosa*. These eating disorders arise from a complex interaction of anxiety, depression, issues of life, and concern over body image that converge into compulsive and often highly dangerous behaviors that can rob an adolescent of health or life itself.

Some people with eating disorders (especially adolescents) have been known to share "tricks of the trade" with one another. But a more disturbing development over the past several years has been the emergence of Web sites proclaiming anorexia and bulimia to be positive lifestyles and not disorders. Posting "Thin Commandments" (such as "Being thin is more important than being healthy" and "Being thin and not eating are signs of true willpower and success"), bingeing and purging tips, and "thinspiration" stories, these sites offer an unsettling look into the mindset of those who are not interested in "recovering" from their ongoing behavior.

Because eating disorders can put health and even life in serious jeopardy, they should be taken very seriously. Initiating treatment can be difficult for the bulimic, who hides so much of her disordered behavior, and for the anorexic, who may stubbornly deny that she needs help and undermine (or vigorously oppose) therapeutic efforts.

In order to be effective, treatment must address a variety of issues and will often require a team approach. A thorough medical evaluation is extremely important and will sometimes reveal a variety of problems that need attention. Counseling will be needed on a long-term basis and should involve the entire family. Antidepressant medication that normalizes neurotransmitter levels can help stabilize mood, relieve depression, and reduce the obsessive component of anorexia. A dietitian should also be involved to provide nutritional input and accountability. Pastoral counseling (ideally by someone who has some familiarity with eating disorders) can help address issues of guilt and shame, as well as critical worldview and spiritual issues, especially for those who see their eating behavior as a means of achieving self-mastery and perfection. In severe cases of anorexia, hospitalization and medically supervised refeeding may be necessary to prevent a fatal outcome.

It is impossible to predict who might develop an eating disorder, but it *is* possible for parents to reduce an adolescent's risk in the following ways:

Beware of perfectionism, especially in regard to a child's weight or physical appearance. Your child must understand that her worth and your acceptance of her are not based on physical beauty or perfect performance but are, in fact, unconditional. If you have difficulty expressing this idea to your child or adolescent, you might need to address this issue in counseling on your own.

Beware of demands on an adolescent to "make weight" for an athletic team, slim down for a cheerleading or dance team, or in some other way subject the body to stringent dietary restrictions for any reason.

Help your child understand that body shape and build have a strong genetic basis and that few women are capable of attaining cover-girl status, even with intense effort.

Eliminate from your own and your family's conversations jokes or other demeaning comments about the appearance of others.

Point out to your children how advertising and other media put forth images of beauty and body image that are out of reach for nearly everyone.

Be a good role model in your own eating and exercise habits, and be careful about openly criticizing your own body appearance.

Focus on relationships and building emotional intimacy in your family, rather than on food-related issues. Be aware of the purposes beyond relieving hunger that food might be serving in your home. Is it used for comfort or reward? Is it used to relieve boredom? Be careful not to use food as a substitute for hugs and saying "I love you."

—Paul C. Reisser, M.D.[7]

Chapter 4

HIGH TECH, LOW STANDARDS

In the mid-1950s, television had no more than 12 channels, the content of movies was constrained by a code of strictly enforced values, the top 10 songs on the radio dealt with "moons and Junes," and the most provocative game in the toy store was Monopoly.

Today, material containing crude language, intense violence (including scenes of mutilation and torture), casual nudity, explicit sex, and general disrespect for life and traditional values is readily accessible to anyone, including children. Network television's "family hour" programs routinely explore themes that would have knocked the first generation of viewers out of their chairs.

A couple of clicks of the remote control or the mouse can deliver hard-core pornography to your TV screen or your child's computer monitor. A number of electronic games not only include this type of content but also offer children and teenagers vicarious participation in antisocial and criminal activity.

Even more troubling has been the explosive growth of Internet sites that allow children to expose themselves to a vast audience, both verbally and visually, in ways that are highly inappropriate. And while violent or sexually explicit sights and sounds create strong and disturbing memories, repeated exposure has a desensitizing effect that can warp attitudes and erode respect for the human body—and life itself.

Unless you cut your family off from civilization altogether, you will need to be perpetually vigilant about the material your child sees and hears, and you should be prepared to deal with whatever leaks past your defenses. More important, you need to do this in a way that prepares your children to make mature, informed decisions about their listening and viewing habits after they leave home. They won't watch *Sesame Street* reruns forever.

—Paul C. Reisser, M.D.[8]

Identifying Your Needs

1. The last time you inquired into your child's media diet,
   a. you were pleased with his entertainment choices.
   b. you were told to submit the proper forms to his attorney.
   c. a "facebook" was still a compilation of photos depicting high school students with embarrassing hairstyles.
   d. other _____

2. Your child's favorite recording artist is
   a. a contemporary Christian musician.
   b. a controversial secular singer.
   c. in rehab.
   d. other _____

3. If your child could watch only one TV show, it would be
   a. *Dora the Explorer.*
   b. *Dog the Bounty Hunter.*
   c. your dream come true.
   d. other _____

4. By playing video games, your child has learned
   a. outstanding eye-hand coordination.

b. how to shoot people without remorse.

c. the absolute limits of your patience.

d. other _____

5. When it comes to using technology, you set the example by

a. never posting threats or gossip on Internet forums.

b. never downloading pirated movies or music.

c. never sticking a fork into a surge protector.

d. other _____

6. As far as you're concerned, technology is

a. bringing parents and children together.

b. driving parents and children apart.

c. anything that was invented after you were born.

d. other _____

CATCHING THE VISION

Watching and Discussing the DVD

Smartphones, Blu-ray, MP3 downloads, social networking Web sites—by the time you read this, these may have gone the way of the eight-track tape. Technology has been with us since the invention of the sharp stick, and it will continue to morph and entertain and shape the way our children think and act.

Unfortunately, not all of that shaping will be positive. From violent video games to Internet porn to the sheer number of hours spent staring at screens and pushing buttons, misused technology threatens to stunt our kids' emotional, mental, spiritual, and physical growth. In this DVD segment, experts offer solutions for concerned but busy parents.

Ron Luce of Teen Mania Ministries returns with a look at how young people are affected by today's entertainment and technology.

Dr. Archibald Hart, former dean of the School of Psychology at Fuller Theological Seminary and author of more than two dozen books including *Sleep, It Does a Family Good* (Focus on the Family/Tyndale, 2010), says technology is overstimulating hormone production, blocking learning, and disrupting sleep.

Rebecca Hagelin, senior communications fellow at the Heritage Foundation whose books include *Home Invasion: Protecting Your Family in a Culture That's Gone Stark Raving Mad* (Thomas Nelson, 2009), believes most parents don't know what their kids are up to when they're watching those screens and pushing those buttons.

In this session, though, you'll find out.

After viewing the DVD, use questions like these to help you think through what you saw and heard.

1. When you compare the presentations of Dr. Archibald Hart, Rebecca Hagelin, and Ron Luce,
   - which person do you think uses technology most often? Why?
   - which person would you rather have watching over your shoulder while you're on the Internet? Why?
   - which person do you think has the most urgent message? Why?
   - which person's advice applies most to your family at this moment? Why?

2. Which of the following have you seen symptoms of in your home? How many seem connected to your family's use of technology and media? How do you feel about that?
   - sleep deprivation
   - short attention spans
   - mild depression
   - loss of face-to-face social time
   - other _____

3. Which of the following measures do you think would help your family? Which one might help most? How long would it take to make that change?
    - Make sure your kids have enough "down time."
    - Schedule no more than an hour in the late afternoon for using technology.
    - Keep evening activities socially oriented.
    - Keep computers, video game consoles, etc. out of the child's bedroom.
    - Use cell phones in an open area where you can be held accountable.
    - Include more "natural" activities like sports and building things.
    - Believe that your kids want your company, even if they seem satisfied with electronics.

4. Which of the following would you describe as common sense? Uncommon sense? Nonsense? Why?
    - Teens want to spend time with their families, even though they spend up to eight hours a day with pop culture.
    - If parents knew how important their influence is, they wouldn't give it up to the media.
    - If your kids are watching something questionable on TV and you walk by in silence, you're sending the message that it's okay.
    - Know how to get into your child's social networking sites.
    - Use a good Internet filter.
    - Marketers are luring kids with highly sexualized material and romanticized rebellion.
    - It's a different world now; you can't raise kids the way your parents did.

5. When it comes to technology, how do some parents turn their homes into the "no-zone"? Which of the following limits do you believe are reasonable, and which enter the "no-zone"?
   - Don't talk to strangers online.
   - No cell phones on Sunday night because Monday is a school day.
   - No social networking sites unless you give Mom and Dad your passwords.
   - No technology an hour or less before bedtime.
   - No more than a total of one hour a day for TV, Internet, and video games.

Bible Study

> *Have nothing to do with the fruitless deeds of darkness, but rather expose them. For it is shameful even to mention what the disobedient do in secret. (Ephesians 5:11-12)*

1. Does your child tend to find "the fruitless deeds of darkness" entertaining or shameful? How do you know?

> *Avoid it, do not travel on it;*
> *turn from it and go on your way.*
> *For they cannot sleep till they do evil;*
> *they are robbed of slumber till they make someone fall.*
> *They eat the bread of wickedness*
> *and drink the wine of violence.*
> *The path of the righteous is like the first gleam of dawn,*

shining ever brighter till the full light of day.
But the way of the wicked is like deep darkness;
they do not know what makes them stumble.
My son, pay attention to what I say;
listen closely to my words.
Do not let them out of your sight,
keep them within your heart;
for they are life to those who find them
and health to a man's whole body.
Above all else, guard your heart,
for it is the wellspring of life.
Put away perversity from your mouth;
keep corrupt talk far from your lips.
Let your eyes look straight ahead,
fix your gaze directly before you.
Make level paths for your feet
and take only ways that are firm.
Do not swerve to the right or the left;
keep your foot from evil.
My son, pay attention to my wisdom,
listen well to my words of insight,
that you may maintain discretion
and your lips may preserve knowledge.
For the lips of an adulteress drip honey,
and her speech is smoother than oil;
but in the end she is bitter as gall,
sharp as a double-edged sword.
Her feet go down to death;
her steps lead straight to the grave.
She gives no thought to the way of life;
her paths are crooked, but she knows it not. (Proverbs 4:15–5:6)

2. Underline any words or phrases in Proverbs 4:15–5:6 that remind you of current Internet sites, TV shows, movies, video games, or music. Then jot down any advice you think would be worth passing on to your child.

I will set before my eyes
no vile thing.
The deeds of faithless men I hate;
they will not cling to me. (Psalm 101:3)

3. If your child adopted this philosophy, how might it affect his viewing of TV, the Internet, video games, and films?

Finally, brothers, whatever is true, whatever is noble, whatever is right, whatever is pure, whatever is lovely, whatever is admirable—if anything is excellent or praiseworthy—think about such things. (Philippians 4:8)

4. Based on this verse, what current TV show, movie, Web site, or album do you think would be worth your child's time this week?

Blessed is the man
*   who does not walk in the counsel of the wicked*
*   or stand in the way of sinners*
*   or sit in the seat of mockers.*
But his delight is in the law of the LORD,
and on his law he meditates day and night.
He is like a tree planted by streams of water,
which yields its fruit in season
and whose leaf does not wither.

Whatever he does prospers.
Not so the wicked!
They are like chaff
that the wind blows away.
(Psalm 1:1-4)

5. Have you tried to replace any inappropriate parts of your child's media diet with alternatives that emphasize "the law of the Lord"? If so, what happened? If not, do you think this is an approach worth trying?

Applying the Principles

1. Here are some questions that may help you engage your child and crack open the door to media discernment. Choose four to ask your child this week after you've watched one of her favorite shows, gone to one of her favorite Web sites, or listened together to some of her favorite music.

    ___ What is it about this form of entertainment that attracts you? Why do you like it more than others?

    ___ Why do you listen or watch? (If it's simply because friends do, ask, "Why do your friends listen to or watch it?")

    ___ How does this form of entertainment make you feel?

    ___ Do the themes reflect reality? Do they reflect truth? If they reflect reality, do they also gloss over evil?

    ___ What are the major, minor, and subtle messages being conveyed through this entertainment? Do you agree or disagree with them?

___ Do you think some people might take these messages literally? What positive things could that lead to? Negative?

___ How do the messages compare with the values you've been taught here at home, or in church?

___ Do you think these messages have any effect on how close you feel to your family, friends, or God? Why or why not?

___ Would you feel comfortable if Jesus sat here listening to or watching this with you (see Matthew 28:20)? Do you think He'd be concerned, or would He enjoy it?

___ Does this entertainment reflect an opinion about God? What is it?

___ What would happen if you imitated the lifestyles and choices of the characters in these songs or this program?

___ What do you consider to be inappropriate entertainment? Where do you draw the line? Where does Scripture draw the line? Are they the same?

___ How does it make you feel to know that, by purchasing a CD, going to a movie, watching a TV show, etc., you are supporting the ideas being promoted?

2. If your teen has inappropriate music or videos in his collection, which of the following steps will you take?

   a. Pray that he'll voluntarily purge the junk from his playlist and movie library.

   b. Accept responsibility for taking too long to "set the boundaries" and agree to replace the offenders with ones that meet the family standard.

    c. Try to sell the products at a garage sale, on eBay, or elsewhere.

    d. Buy the stuff from your teen and destroy it.

    e. Try to return the material to the store.

    f. other _____

3. Which of the following would be most helpful to your family as you make entertainment and technology choices this week?

    a. paying more attention to movie ratings and "Parental Advisory" stickers

    b. reading reviews at www.pluggedin.com

    c. asking, "What would Jesus do?"

    d. getting rid of your TV

    e. other _____

4. Which of the following would help you become a better role model when it comes to media discernment?

    a. spending less time on the Internet

    b. being more careful about videos you rent or buy

    c. pointing out positive things about movies you've seen

    d. playing a different radio station in the car

    e. spending less time on your cell phone

    f. other _____

5. On the next page is a sample form you can use as a guideline to compose your own standard of what's acceptable in your home. Although it avoids the specifics, you'll want to be as specific as you can so that family members understand (and agree to) the boundaries.

Our Family Constitution for Acceptable Media

As family members committed to the lordship of Jesus Christ and wanting to live out personal holiness as He commands, we pledge from this day forward to honor God in our media choices. Despite poor decisions that may have been made in the past, we want the blessings that come from obedience. Because we realize that certain types of entertainment are spiritually unhealthy, we ask God to guide and strengthen us as we work to make good entertainment choices, empowered by the fruit of the Spirit (self-control—our part) and the ongoing work of the Holy Spirit (His part).

Knowing that God commands us to "above all else, guard your heart" (Proverbs 4:23), we pledge to guard it from harmful influences that work against our faith.

We agree to avoid all forms of entertainment (music, film, video, Internet, magazines, books, television, video games, etc.) that _____.

In the rare event one of us feels an exception to the above should be made, we pledge to bring this issue and the possible reasons for it to the family to discuss and evaluate, rather than make this decision in isolation.

We understand that signing this "family constitution" has no bearing on our salvation (which is 100 percent dependent upon our faith in Jesus Christ as Savior and Lord), but is an outgrowth of our desire to please God and obey Him in every area of our lives.

Family members sign below:

_____   _____

_____   _____

_____   _____

Date _____

Insight for Your Week

What can you do to help your kids make better lifelong choices in entertainment? Feel free to adapt and apply the following suggestions in your home.

1. Keep the main thing the main thing. Not all entertainment is "hollow and deceptive" (Colossians 2:8), but much of it is. Some kids—even Christian kids—willingly allow themselves to be taken "captive" by the world.

For these young people, teaching media discernment is getting the cart before the horse. What they need first is to give Jesus Christ the foremost priority in their lives.

2. Know your kids' entertainment. Find out what entertainment picks are spinning inside your child's head. With pen and paper and a listening ear, ask about your child's favorite five musicians. Then list the movies and TV shows your son or daughter says are the most exciting and engaging. Follow that up by asking about his top five Internet sites.

Refrain from jumping in and playing judge and jury at this point. Listen, listen, and listen some more. There will be a time to offer your views, but not during this exploratory stage.

If you discover entertainment choices that concern you, schedule a follow-up time to discuss them. This will give you a chance to mull over how you're going to broach the subject (and give you time to pray).

3. Set a family standard. Each family must decide together where to draw the line, using scriptural principles as a guide. Factor in an understanding of each family member's maturity, critical thinking skills, and commitment to holiness. Don't forget prayer.

Go to great lengths, if necessary, to find common ground with your child on media standards. Keep leading him or her back to important Bible verses and asking what conclusions he or she draws from them.

Now articulate your family's decisions in writing. Develop a "family constitution" dealing with entertainment habits in your home.

If your child is already a fan of questionable media, you face a special challenge. You can start operating under the new standard "from this day forward," but you—and preferably your child—must determine how to deal with the garbage festering in his or her entertainment collection. Here are some possible scenarios:

- After discovering the need for discernment, your child may voluntarily purge the junk from his music and movie library, as well as change his TV viewing habits.
- You can humbly accept responsibility for taking too long to "set the boundaries" and agree to replace the offenders with ones that meet the family standard.
- A local pawn shop might pay two or three bucks apiece for the discs, videos, and video games you're anxious to get rid of. Since you probably don't want to put these products back into circulation, you might agree to purchase them from your child at the same rate and then break out the sledgehammer and the Hefty bag. (Hey, they're yours now. You can do anything you want with them!)
- If you have one or two "out of bounds" products still in nearly new condition, you can try returning them to the store that sold them. Some retailers will refund the purchase price—or offer store credit— to a parent who makes a return because of offensive content.

After you've established family standards and weeded out everything that flunks the test, you're ready to start fresh. Hold firm to the new guidelines. From now on, if your child asks to purchase a certain media product, you can say, "Sure, but when you bring it home, we'll review it together. If we can't agree that it meets the family standard, you'll have to get rid of it. You'll be out the money."

Rest assured: If your child knows it's his money on the line, he'll be much more selective about which entertainers he invites home.

4. Be wary of extremes. At one extreme, some moms and dads choose to "lay down the law": No movies, no television, no secular music, period. While this approach may seem to simplify things, it may also breed rebellion if you haven't taken the time to convince your child that it's reasonable. Young people bide their time, waiting for the day they can sample the entertainment industry's forbidden fruit: "Just wait till I move out— I'll watch and listen to whatever I want."

Other parents go to the opposite extreme, adopting an anything-goes philosophy. This permissive approach leads to "indecent exposure" as children wander, aimless and wide-eyed, through the culture's enticements.

Neither of these extremes works for most families. A discerning middle ground—one that tests entertainment against biblical standards—is the more reasonable and protective plan of action.

5. Don't judge on style or ratings. Trusting a rating system is like buying a used car solely on the basis of a classified ad that boasts, "Great car." Who decided? Based on what criteria? Though it takes a little more research, it's worth your time and effort to go beyond the rating and find out about a show's content.

Likewise, musical styles can be deceptive. While "harder" genres can offer positive messages, some mellower musicians dump lyrical sewage on their fans. Check out the message being conveyed, not just the style or look of the messenger.

6. Check out the ride ahead of time. Who has time to prescreen every movie, CD, and televised program? Fortunately, there are inexpensive (sometimes free), trustworthy media-review resources that can help.

Plugged In, for example, gives concise reviews of what's hot in the media. You can reach this resource online at www.pluggedin.com.

7. Ask: WWJD? While the fad may have faded, the principle behind the "What Would Jesus Do?" products will never dim. By encouraging our teens to use the "WWJD?" principle in the area of media choices, we can teach them how to fish in this media-saturated culture.

8. Model wise choices. One of the surest ways to derail your young person's media discernment is to act hypocritically. Nothing lasting can be accomplished if teaching discernment amounts to a parent saying, "No watching MTV in this house," while viewing *The Sopranos* on DVD.

9. Don't lose hope. Perhaps you have a child who just doesn't get it. Don't despair. There really is hope. It may be a matter of finding the right book or tape or CD that specifically addresses today's media. Or encourage your teen to attend a seminar on the subject at a church or youth conference.

10. Fight the spiritual battle. Helping our kids to have fun without being victimized by the wrong kinds of media messages doesn't just happen. It takes a "fight" to succeed.

We're in a battle—a spiritual fray for the hearts and minds of our young people. Fighting for this high ground is not optional—it's essential for their well-being and protection.

—Bob Waliszewski and Bob Smithouser[9]

Chapter 5

TEACHING A TRUE VIEW

A professor lectured at a political science class in Boulder, Colorado, where 250 students were learning the judicial history of the United States. Their minds were sharp, and they were beginning to formulate their opinions on courts, laws, attorneys, and the issues that are worth fighting for. They were ready for the professor's question: "Can any of you in this class tell me that Adolf Hitler was morally wrong by doing what he did in World War II?"

To his astonishment, not one hand went up.

He continued, "Are there any Jews in this classroom?"

One young woman on the front row raised her hand.

He walked over to her and said, "In effect, you are telling me that a man who killed 6 million Jewish people in one of the largest genocides in history isn't morally wrong. Are you saying you cannot find fault with a man who hung his own men by piano wire and watched them squirm while the wire slowly cut their throats? Are you telling me that a man who ordered vivisection on infants to learn how to effectively kill the human body is not morally wrong?"

She looked up at him with confidence and said, "In my opinion, what he did was wrong, but I will not stand and make a moral judgment on him."

Moral judgments in our society have become the hallmark of bad character. If someone decides to stand up for what's right, he is immediately ostracized from society and treated as if he were the cause of all the hate in the world.

Yet we must stand up and identify right from wrong. Ideas like those of Hitler have consequences.

The consequences of wrong ideas in your child's life can be disastrous, too. A lack of standards can lead to promiscuity and abortion, drugs and other addictions, aimlessness, despair, and suicide.

Without a clear vision of the world as God made it, we are all doomed. Having a Christian worldview, however, provides that clear vision.

—Andy Braner[10]

Identifying Your Needs

1. What have you done so far to teach your child a Christian worldview?
   a. Sent him to seminary while the other kids were playing softball.
   b. Made sure there's a Bible under his pillow each night while he sleeps.
   c. Given him a brain transplant.
   d. other _____

2. You can tell whether a person sees the world through a biblical lens by
   a. observing whether he loves his neighbor.
   b. asking him whether Scripture is inerrant.
   c. lighting up a cigarette and seeing if he runs away.
   d. other _____

3. What part of a Christian worldview is hardest for you to understand?
   a. the nature of the Trinity

b. how theology relates to economics

c. whether dogs go to heaven

d. other _____

4. What part of a Christian worldview would be hardest for you to instill in your child?

a. the need for evangelism in a culture of diversity

b. the reality of spiritual warfare

c. not playing games on your iPhone in church

d. other _____

5. If two Christians have different worldviews, what should they do?

a. Examine the Scriptures together.

b. Agree to disagree.

c. Pound each other with copies of *Strong's Exhaustive Concordance*.

d. other _____

6. If your child questions what you've taught him about God, it's best to

a. encourage him to find answers.

b. have him deprogrammed immediately.

c. tell him, "When in doubt, just get out."

d. other _____

CATCHING THE VISION

Watching and Discussing the DVD

In this DVD segment, Dr. Del Tackett and Dr. Michelle Anthony tackle a problem many parents face—even though they may not realize it. It's their children's lack of a biblical worldview, and it affects every aspect of their kids' lives.

As author and teacher for Focus on the Family's The Truth Project®, a nationwide initiative designed to bring the Christian worldview to the body of Christ, Del knows the importance of helping kids see life through the Bible's lenses. So does Michelle, a pastor of family ministries and author of *Spiritual Parenting* (David C. Cook, 2010).

Children are shaped by what they believe. In a society less and less convinced that absolute truth exists, how can we fortify our kids to swim upstream? How can we teach them confidently without being dogmatic or haughty? It starts with examining our own words and actions—and practicing humility.

After viewing the DVD, use questions like these to help you think through what you saw and heard.

1. If this video were the only thing you'd ever seen about this subject, what might be your definition of "Christian worldview"? How might you respond to its call to cultivate such a worldview in your children?

2. What does it mean to "compartmentalize" your faith? Which of the following "compartments" do you think most Christian kids tend to keep separate from their beliefs about Jesus?
   - school
   - eating
   - career goals
   - video games
   - music
   - friendships
   - politics
   - sports
   - money

3. Dr. Del Tackett has urged Christians to be confident but not arrogant when they talk about truth. How could you rephrase each of the following to be less dogmatic and more humble?

- "Evolutionists reject God because they don't want to have to obey Him."
- "People who think abortion should be allowed are murderers."
- "Followers of false religions are really following the devil."
- "Wearing your baseball cap in the church building is a sin."
- "Everybody should get married."

4. When teaching a biblical worldview, it's important to speak the truth in an age-appropriate way. How could you rephrase each of the following so that your child could understand it?
   - "We commemorate Jesus' crucifixion with Communion."
   - "God is omniscient, omnipresent, and eternal."
   - "Noah found favor in the eyes of the Lord."
   - "We are redeemed by the blood of the Lamb."

5. Do you agree with all of the following? Why or why not? What's one way in which each statement could affect the way you parent this week?
   - Today's kids are being hammered with the notion of tolerance.
   - We have to work hard to show truth rather than just speak it.
   - It's more important to teach discernment than to lay down a lot of don'ts.
   - Legalism has led more people away from Christianity than anything else.
   - Grace and love are risky because our kids might walk away.

Bible Study

He is the image of the invisible God, the firstborn over all creation.
For by him all things were created: things in heaven and on earth, visible
and invisible, whether thrones or powers or rulers or authorities; all

things were created by him and for him. He is before all things, and in him all things hold together. (Colossians 1:15-17)

1. If everything is "held together" by Christ, what will understanding Christianity help your child to do?

   We demolish arguments and every pretension that sets itself up against the knowledge of God, and we take captive every thought to make it obedient to Christ. (2 Corinthians 10:5)

2. Has your child encountered anti-Christian arguments at school, on TV, or elsewhere? How do you know? What happened?

   Does this verse imply that we should attack those who don't have a Christian worldview? Explain.

   One of them, an expert in the law, tested him with this question: "Teacher, which is the greatest commandment in the Law?" Jesus replied: " 'Love the Lord your God with all your heart and with all your soul and with all your mind.' " (Matthew 22:35-37)

3. What does it mean to love God with all your mind?

   Has the emphasis of your child's spiritual training been on thinking or feeling? Are you satisfied with that?

   See to it that no one takes you captive through hollow and deceptive philosophy, which depends on human tradition and the basic principles of this world rather than on Christ. (Colossians 2:8)

4. How do you suppose your child would summarize his philosophy of life in 25 words or less? Would it depend more on human wisdom or biblical truth?

Do not conform any longer to the pattern of this world, but be transformed by the renewing of your mind. Then you will be able to test and approve what God's will is—his good, pleasing and perfect will. (Romans 12:2)

5. What's one thing a parent could do to help a child "renew" her mind?

Applying the Principles

1. Try answering each of the following questions in 25 words or less.

   How do you know God really created the world?

   How do you know the Bible is true?

   This week ask your child, if he or she is old enough, to answer those questions—and compare your replies. In which of these areas do you need the most help? In which does your child need the most help?

2. If your child asked, "Why should I care about having a Christian worldview?" which of the following answers might make the most sense to him or her?
   - a. "If you're a Christian, you need a Christian worldview."
   - b. "Other worldviews aren't true."
   - c. "Without the right foundation, you can get into all sorts of trouble."
   - d. "Because I said so."
   - e. other _____

3. How could each of the following be an opportunity to talk with your child about having a Christian worldview?

   watching a TV news story about abortion protesters being arrested

   discovering that someone has bumped into your car in the parking lot and driven away

   visiting your terminally ill uncle together in a nursing home

4. In which of the following places are you most likely to have a chance to discuss your child's worldview this week?
   a. going to or from church
   b. at the dinner table
   c. in front of the TV
   d. while taking a walk
   e. other _____

5. Which of the following issues do you think you need to address first with your child?
   a. what God is like
   b. God's role in the creation of the universe
   c. the existence of absolute truth
   d. who Jesus is
   e. people's need to be reconciled to God
   f. other _____

6. In order to address the issue(s) you just chose, how will you need to get ready?

   Who (spouse, friend, pastor, etc.) could help you prepare?

Insight for Your Week

What happens if your child fails to develop a solid Christian worldview? He'll be stuck with the wrong map. If you try to use the wrong map, you're lost! And lost people tend to end up in dangerous neighborhoods.

When your mind goes unprotected by a comprehensive, biblical perspective, you're a sitting duck for misleading ideas that could cost you your life. At the very least, you'll end up thinking and living like those around you who are without God—instead of like a follower of Jesus Christ.

Where to begin?

If your child is old enough, here are some worldview questions you can ask him right now. They'll help you grasp what kind of teachings he has been assimilating.

1. *What is God?*
   a. Is there a God?
   b. Is God personal or impersonal?
   c. Are there many gods?

2. *What is man?*
   a. Why do you wake up in the morning?
   b. What are your long-term goals in life?
   c. Is mankind an evolutionary step to another being?
   d. Was mankind created to worship God?

3. *What is your ultimate purpose in life?*
   a. Is your purpose in life to experience the most pleasure you can at all times?

      b. Is your purpose in life to understand how the mind and body
        work together to overcome trials and struggles?

      c. Is your purpose to know and serve the God of the Bible?

      d. Is your purpose to be rich, powerful, or famous?

4. *Where do you find truth?*

      a. Is truth a relative explanation of events?

      b. Is truth found in yourself?

      c. Is truth found in the Bible?

      d. Is truth found in any other religious work as well?

Once you've had those initial conversations to determine where your child is, the fun really begins. Let's review several fundamental truths, or cornerstones, of a Christian worldview.

1. God is a personal being. The Christian worldview is unique: God is a real, supernatural being who desires a personal relationship with man.

2. The breath of God formed the world. The Bible says plainly, "In the beginning God created the heavens and the earth" (Genesis 1:1). Then He made humans in His image.

If God created people, how should we deal with the issue of euthanasia? Should we intentionally kill people who no longer give anything back to society? How should we view Alzheimer's, AIDS, or any other terminal illness?

3. Human nature aspires to perfection. People are attracted to what is perfect. But if your child thinks material possessions will make his life perfect, then the latest car, the biggest house, and the most expensive toys will be his pursuit.

The Christian pursues Christlikeness, which is as perfect as you can be. How would your kids' lives change if they wanted to be as perfect as Christ? What kind of movies would they watch? What would be their view of material possessions?

4. Absolute truth is found in God. Many people today say that ultimate truth is a figment of our imagination. The Christian worldview, on the other hand, says there is absolute, objective truth, and its source is God.

5. *Jesus Christ is the Son of God.* Some people call Jesus a good teacher. Some call Him a prophet. Some say He is the best example of a man who incorporated His own godhood in daily life. Scripture calls Him the Son of God.

6. *Evil is a result of man's sin.* The apostle Paul wrote, "Sin entered the world through one man, and death through sin, and in this way death came to all men, because all sinned" (Romans 5:12). When your kids grasp the consequences of sin in their lives, they will be able to appreciate the forgiveness God has offered them.

7. *Jesus came to die on account of our sin and reconcile us to God.* "Since death came through a man, the resurrection of the dead comes also through a man" (1 Corinthians 15:21). That man is Jesus.

Passing on a Christian worldview is not as simple as sitting your children down for a series of lectures or family devotions. Boring your kids will hurt your cause anyway.

A far better approach is found in Deuteronomy 11:18-19: "Fix these words of mine in your hearts and minds; tie them as symbols on your hands and bind them on your foreheads. Teach them to your children, talking about them when you sit at home and when you walk along the road, when you lie down and when you get up."

Every casual dinner conversation, every movie or TV show you watch together, every drive to the store or hike in nature is rife with opportunities to discuss some aspect of the Christian worldview.

Make it a priority to reinforce the Christian worldview with your kids. With that map, they will walk with God, avoid dangerous detours, and reach their destination.

—Andy Braner[11]

Chapter 6

DON'T JUST SAY NO

My wife, Janet, and I actively try to know our children's friends. We talk to our teens about who they "hang" with at school, church youth group, and sports events. We seek to understand the hot topics they're discussing. And we're very old-fashioned: We want to know where they're going, whom they're going to be with, and what time they'll be home. If they miss curfew, they know they will be grounded.

I tell them I also reserve the right to show up at any place they tell me they're going. This could be a sporting event, party, or a friend's house. I don't do that out of a lack of trust, but as a loving parent who knows there are situations in a teen's life that aren't always what they seem to be. Your teen can be expecting a simple gathering with friends for a movie but have it turn out to be a beer bust in a house where no adults are present.

My teens and I sometimes differ over what needs to be considered in their plans: Are the parents going to be home? Who else will be there? When is the party going to end? How will you get home? Some parents don't share your values and will actually buy alcohol and drugs for their kids. My intent is to be a safety net for my children and to provide as many ways out of any bad situation as possible.

I remember when I was in high school and went to a party after a football game. I told my dad where the party was and that the parents would be home. They were there, all right, and they bought the keg!

They believed this was okay since they were there to supervise the drinking. They weren't thinking about the drive home or the other parents' values.

Well, my dad sensed something wasn't right, and he came to the party unannounced. He wanted to meet and talk with the parents. I was in the basement when someone told me my dad was upstairs. Immediately I got rid of the beer, went upstairs, and faced my dad as though nothing were wrong. I really didn't want him going to the basement! He simply told me it was time to go home.

I left with my dad. I wasn't upset, because I knew that what I had been doing was wrong. If I had told him he had embarrassed me and that I felt he didn't trust me, he would have said I was right. I had just proved I couldn't be trusted by choosing to go against our house rules. If there had been no alcohol at the party, he would have simply visited with the parents and not bothered me. As it was, he had made a strong statement to my friends, their parents, and me: He would exercise his right as my father to show up when and if he felt something was amiss. His primary goal was to protect me because he loved me.

—Jim Weidmann[12]

Identifying Your Needs

1. When you were growing up, you chose friends by
    a. asking them whether they were Christians.
    b. flipping a coin.
    c. handing out dollar bills to likely prospects on the school
       bus.
    d. other _____

2. Who had the strongest positive influence on you when you were a young person?
    a. your parents
    b. a youth worker at church
    c. the cast of *High School Musical*
    d. other _____

3. You screen your child's friends by
    a. employing private detectives.
    b. using a lie detector.
    c. asking them to name the kings of Judah in alphabetical order.
    d. other _____

4. When it comes to alcohol,
    a. you have a zero tolerance policy.
    b. you hope your child won't repeat your mistakes.
    c. you're very careful not to drink in front of people from your church.
    d. other _____

5. If you suspected that your child was using an illegal drug, you would
    a. ransack her room.
    b. give her a drug test.
    c. sign up for a reality TV show.
    d. other _____

6. Peer pressure is
    a. a myth.
    b. unavoidable, universal, and deadly.
    c. the compulsion to squint when trying to read fine print.
    d. other _____

Watching and Discussing the DVD

Some parents think drug and alcohol abuse is only about a few "misfits" who drop out of school and spend all their time in a stupor. But what about steroid-injecting sports heroes, "pharm parties," and weekend binge drinking? Kids in our society are introduced to the idea of substance abuse at an early age—even if they aren't introduced to the substances themselves until later.

Glenn Williams knows it's vital to talk to children—even younger ones—about drugs, alcohol, and the temptation to use both. He's a psychologist licensed in Australia and author of *Talking Smack: Who's Talking to Your Kids about Drugs and Alcohol, If You're Not?* (Authentic, 2010). In this DVD segment, he's joined by Daniel Huerta, licensed clinical social worker and counselor for Focus on the Family. Together they address drinking, smoking, and drugs—and the peer pressure and other influences that cause kids to experiment dangerously.

What are we teaching our children about these substances through our example—and through the conversations we may *not* be having? It's time to face the discomfort we may feel and start talking with our kids about choosing healthier, happier futures.

After viewing the DVD, use questions like these to help you think through what you saw and heard.

1. When you see messages on TV or elsewhere urging parents to talk with their kids about drugs or alcohol, what's your reaction? Why?
   - *I'm not qualified to do that.*
   - *My kid will never do that stuff anyway.*
   - *I can't find the time.*
   - *I did that once; it was enough.*
   - *He'd just roll his eyes.*

- *Mind your own business.*
- *I'll get around to it—someday.*
- other _____

2. How would you rank the following influences (strongest to weakest) on your child's choices to use or avoid alcohol, tobacco, and drugs?
    - seeing a sports team celebrate victory with champagne
    - being invited to a party where beer is served
    - going to Sunday school or church youth group
    - watching anti-smoking ads on TV
    - observing your use of painkillers for minor headaches
    - hearing that a favorite musician died of a drug overdose
    - seeing you drink coffee every morning "to wake up"
    - reading that a favorite actor is in alcohol rehab
    - knowing that a best friend smokes
    - other _____

3. How would you sum up the message of the DVD presentation?
    - "Just say no."
    - "Parents: the anti-drug."
    - "Meth: not even once."
    - "This is your brain on drugs."
    - "Drink responsibly."
    - "Get high on life."
    - other _____

4. Forget the clichés about peer pressure. How might a conversation *really* go in which your child is pressured by a peer to try marijuana? Where and when do you envision such a conversation taking place? On a scale of 1 to 10 (10 highest), how prepared do you think your child is for that conversation?

5. How do you measure success when it comes to steering kids away from harmful use of alcohol and other drugs? Which of the following comes closest to your goal? What step can you take this week toward reaching it?

    - being able to look at my drug-free child 20 years from now
    - being as sure as I can be that, so far, my child has never tried alcohol or drugs
    - keeping my child out of jail
    - knowing that my child has passed a urine test
    - seeing my child denounce drug or alcohol use in a school essay or speech
    - hearing my child urge a friend to stay away from alcohol and drugs
    - other _____

Bible Study

> *Do not be misled: "Bad company corrupts good character."*
> *(1 Corinthians 15:33)*

1. Has your child ever been negatively influenced by a friend? If so, what happened?

    Has your child ever been a "bad influence" on someone else? If so, what happened?

> *Therefore do not be foolish, but understand what the Lord's will is. Do not get drunk on wine, which leads to debauchery. Instead, be filled with the Spirit. (Ephesians 5:17-18)*

2. What's "foolish" about getting drunk? How might you get your child to take the idea of "debauchery" seriously? How about the idea of being filled with the Spirit?

A righteous man is cautious in friendship,
but the way of the wicked leads them astray. (Proverbs 12:26)

3. Do you feel your child has been cautious enough in making friends so far? Why or why not?

Do not be yoked together with unbelievers. For what do righteous-
ness and wickedness have in common? Or what fellowship can light
have with darkness? What harmony is there between Christ and
Belial? What does a believer have in common with an unbeliever?
What agreement is there between the temple of God and idols? For we
are the temple of the living God. As God has said: "I will live with
them and walk among them, and I will be their God, and they will
be my people."
*   "Therefore come out from them*
*   and be separate, says the Lord.*
*   Touch no unclean thing,*
*   and I will receive you." (2 Corinthians 6:14-17)*

4. If 2 Corinthians 6:14-17 were the only passage in the Bible about relating to unbelievers, what would you tell your child about having non-Christian friends?

I have written you in my letter not to associate with sexually im-
moral people—not at all meaning the people of this world who are im-
moral, or the greedy and swindlers, or idolaters. In that case you would
have to leave this world. But now I am writing you that you must not
associate with anyone who calls himself a brother but is sexually immoral

or greedy, an idolater or a slanderer, a drunkard or a swindler. With such
a man do not even eat.

> *What business is it of mine to judge those outside the church? Are*
you not to judge those inside? God will judge those outside. "Expel the
wicked man from among you." (1 Corinthians 5:9-13)

5. How might 1 Corinthians 5:9-13 change your response to the previous question?

Has a *Christian* friend ever been a bad influence on your child? If so, what did you do?

> *After the boy had gone, David got up from the south side of the*
stone and bowed down before Jonathan three times, with his face to the
ground. Then they kissed each other and wept together—but David
wept the most.
>
> *Jonathan said to David, "Go in peace, for we have sworn friend-*
ship with each other in the name of the LORD, saying, 'The LORD is
witness between you and me, and between your descendants and my
descendants forever.'" Then David left, and Jonathan went back to the
town. . . .
>
> *And Saul's son Jonathan went to David at Horesh and helped him*
find strength in God. (1 Samuel 20:41-42; 23:16)

6. What positive spiritual effect did this famous friendship have on David?

Has a friend ever had a similar influence on your child's life? If so, how?

Applying the Principles

1. How well do you know your child's companions? List his or her three best friends below.

    a.

    b.

    c.

   How would you describe the spiritual commitment of each of these friends?

    a.

    b.

    c.

   What additional information do you wish you had about each of these friends?

    a.

    b.

    c.

2. If you need to know more about your child's friends, what steps will you take this week to make that happen?

    a. Ask your child who he "hangs" with at school, church, and elsewhere.

    b. Invite your child's friends over.

    c. Ask a sibling to spy on your child.

    d. other _____

3. Which of the following statements are true of you?

    a. "When my child goes somewhere, I know who he's going to be with and what time he'll be home."

        ____ always

        ____ sometimes

        ____ seldom

        ____ never

    b. "I set penalties for missing curfew and make sure my child knows what they are."

        ____ always

        ____ sometimes

        ____ seldom

        ____ never

    c. "My child knows that I reserve the right to show up at any place he says he's going."

        ____ always

        ____ sometimes

        ____ seldom

        ____ never

4. If your child gets into a compromising or dangerous situation with friends, how will he or she get out of it?

    a. Call or text you on the cell phone you've loaned or given him or her.

    b. Come home in a cab, using the money you've made sure he or she has.

    c. Drive home in the car.

    d. other _____

Have you discussed this plan with your child?

If not, when will you tell him or her about it?

5. The following diagram represents your child's circle of friends. The face in the middle stands for your child. Label the five friends with the names of five kids your child spends time with. Then draw an arrow between your child and each of the others to represent the influence your child has on that friend (or vice versa). If the influence is weak, use a dotted line; if it's strong, use a thick line. If the influence is positive, draw a plus sign next to the arrow; if it's negative, draw a minus.

Now take a look at your diagram. Is there anything about these relationships that concerns you? Is there anything to be thankful for?

If a friend is negatively influencing your child, which of the following steps do you need to take?
   a. Pray.
   b. Warn your child that you'll limit the friendship if the behavior doesn't change.
   c. Tell your child not to spend time with that person anymore.
   d. Move your child to a different school or town.
   e. other _____

Insight for Your Week

How can you talk to kids about risks? Here are nine basic principles.

1. *It's easier to talk about sensitive or difficult subjects if you have good rapport with your child about the easier ones.* Time spent building relationships during the preteen years usually pays major dividends later on.

2. *Parents often worry that if they discuss certain topics (especially sex) in any detail, it will "give the kids ideas."* Here's a late news flash: The kids already have plenty of ideas, and now they need to hear your viewpoint about them. However, they probably won't ask you, so you need to take the initiative.

3. *Warnings about behaviors that threaten life and limb will be more effective if they aren't diluted by nagging about less serious matters.* Accentuate the positive, and what you say about the negative will carry more weight.

4. *Don't expect to communicate your values in a few marathon sessions.* Brief but potent teachable moments crop up regularly throughout childhood and adolescence. Seizing these opportunities requires spending enough time with a child to allow them to take place.

5. *It's easier for an adolescent to stay away from the dangerous detours if the main highway is clearly marked, well lit, attractive, and enjoyable.* Encourage and support healthy goals, commitments, friends, and activities—all of which are strong deterrents to destructive behaviors.

6. *Your actions will reinforce (or invalidate) your words.* The misguided commandment "Do what I say, not what I do" has never worked and never will. However, this doesn't mean that mistakes, miscalculations, and reckless behavior in your past invalidate what you say today. Some parents worry that they can't legitimately warn their kids not to do what they did as teenagers. Heartfelt confessions, cautionary tales, and lessons learned at the University of Hard Knocks can have a profound impact on young listeners. As long as you're not setting a hypocritical double standard ("It's okay for me but not for you"), don't be afraid to share what you've learned the hard way.

7. *Don't shift into "lecture gear" very often, if at all.* Your teenager's desire for independence and his heartfelt need to be treated like an adult (even if his behavior suggests otherwise) will cause eyes to glaze and attention to drift if you launch into a six-point sermon on the evils of _____. If you feel strongly about these issues (and you should), say what's on your heart without beating the point into the ground.

One way to communicate your view indirectly but effectively is through cassette tapes or CDs. You might bring one or more prerecorded messages on a car trip and play them at an appropriate time, perhaps mentioning that they're interesting but not necessarily announcing that you want your adolescent to pay close attention. It helps, of course, if the speaker is engrossing and your teenager isn't plugged into his own portable music device.

8. *Don't give up if your efforts to broach tough topics aren't greeted with enthusiasm.* Even when your tone is open and inviting, you may find that a lively conversation is harder to start than a campfire on a cold, windy night. Your thoughts may be expressed honestly, tactfully, and eloquently, but you still may not get rapt attention from your intended audience. Be patient, don't express frustration, and don't be afraid to try again later. If your spouse has any helpful suggestions about improving your delivery of the messages you care about, listen carefully and act accordingly.

9. *While you state your principles about sex, drugs, and other important matters with consistency, conviction, and clarity, your adolescent also must understand that he can come to you when he has a problem.* If your teenager is convinced that "Mom and Dad will kill me if they find out about _____," you will be the last to find out about it. But if he knows you, like God, are "a refuge and strength, a help in time of trouble," you will be able to help him contain the damage if he makes an unwise decision. And indirectly, you may show him the attributes of God, his ultimate refuge and strength.

—Paul C. Reisser, M.D.[13]

Chapter 7

THE POWER OF A PARENT

Years from now, when your daughter heads off to college or your son moves into his first apartment and you bid her or him farewell with teary eyes, what do you want your child to be able to handle? What kind of foundation would you like him or her to have?

Maybe you've heard the parable of the wise man who built his house upon the rock and the foolish man who built his house upon the sand. Given the choice between the two, sand seems at first the way to go; certainly it's the path of least resistance. It's easier to sink pillars into sand than rock, sand is easy to level, and it usually comes with a great view of the ocean.

But even though a house on the beach might seem like a dream come true, it may be a nightmare in the making: storms and waves might wash away all that you've labored over the years to build. As you watch your house float out to sea, you may think twice about your choice of foundations—which is what I hope you'll do as you think about the foundation you want to build for your child.

Laying a firm foundation doesn't happen overnight. If you want a homegrown child—one who's nurtured at home by involved parents, who has downtime, who is raised for character and not just achievement, who values faith and family—you construct that foundation in layers, day by day.

But the work is worth it. The tremors of childhood and adolescence can shatter other, weaker foundations. A homegrown child will stand firm when she's ridiculed for having big ears, when he gets cut from the team, when her boyfriend breaks up with her and it feels that the ground beneath her is quaking.

A homegrown child has values and lives by them. He has the moxie to stick with it because you've given him Vitamin E—for Encouragement. She has the courage to say "No" because you've given her Vitamin N.

A homegrown child is different—from the inside out.

—Dr. Kevin Leman[14]

Identifying Your Needs

Take a couple of minutes to fill out the following survey.

1. The ultimate purpose of parenting is
    ____ to make your child do the right things.
    ____ to become the person God wants you to be.
    ____ to rid yourself of excess energy and money.
    ____ other _____

2. When parenting doesn't yield the results you want,
    ____ trust God to make things work together for good.
    ____ focus on the journey, not the destination.
    ____ blame it on the Flat Earth Society.
    ____ other _____

3. The most powerful parent you've ever known was
    ____ your mother or father.

_____ your spouse.

_____ the guy who invented disposable diapers.

_____ other _____

4. When people say a parent's role isn't really important, you

_____ wonder why you're working so hard to make a difference.

_____ roll your eyes and snort derisively.

_____ breathe a sigh of relief.

_____ other _____

5. Eating dinner together as a family is a good idea because

_____ you can build relationships and accountability.

_____ you can make sure your kids are getting enough broccoli.

_____ you can steal Tater Tots from each other's plates.

_____ other _____

6. When your child doesn't seem to want you around, you should

_____ hover over him 24/7.

_____ realize that he needs you whether he knows it or not.

_____ go to the Bahamas.

_____ other _____

Watching and Discussing the DVD

In a world of eating disorders, Internet predators, "hooking up," and drunk driving, what's a parent to do? Give up? After all, some "experts" are trying to convince us that the roles of moms and dads aren't important. Genetics and peers, they claim, have the most influence on the choices kids make.

The truth is that *you* are the most important person in your child's life—even if he or she seems to be pulling away. Keep the dialogue going, gently pursuing and studying this emerging individual who is your son or daughter. Your presence says, "I want to walk this road with you."

That's the message of Dr. Juli Slattery, featured in this session's DVD segment. Juli is a family psychologist, author, and broadcast host for Focus on the Family.

Juli is joined by Glenn Williams and Ron Luce, who return to deliver key tips on exercising your power as a parent. They're not rocket science—they're simple things, like eating dinner as a family, staying involved in schoolwork, and spending time with each child.

After viewing the DVD, use questions like these to help you think through what you saw and heard.

1. How might each of the following feel about the idea that parenting doesn't play a very important role in how kids end up?
   - the father of Adolf Hitler
   - the mother of Abraham Lincoln
   - your parents
   - your child

2. If you were paid minimum wage to parent, how much might you have earned last year for each of the following duties? Since you probably weren't paid at all, what was your reward?
   - medical care
   - education
   - housekeeping
   - counseling
   - transportation
   - food service
   - spiritual guidance
   - entertainment

- fire prevention
- juvenile justice
- other _____

3. Based on what you observed in the DVD segment, how do you think Dr. Juli Slattery and Glenn Williams would respond to parents who said the following? How would you respond?
   - "My kids are out of control."
   - "My kids never listen to me."
   - "My kids don't care whether I'm around."
   - "My kids only want my money."

4. How many of the following powerful habits has your family already formed? Which do you think are helping? Which do you think would help if you tried them?
   - eating dinner together
   - doing schoolwork together
   - sharing a hobby
   - spending time with each child individually

5. When do you feel most powerful as a parent? When do you feel weakest? How could memorizing 2 Corinthians 12:9-10 help you at both of those times?

Bible Study

As a mother comforts her child,
so will I comfort you;
and you will be comforted over Jerusalem. (Isaiah 66:13)

As a father has compassion on his children,
so the LORD has compassion on those who fear him. (Psalm 103:13)

1. If mothers and fathers are doing their jobs, what will the atmosphere of their homes be like? How does this affect a parent's ability to influence his or her child?

> *Now Rebekah was listening as Isaac spoke to his son Esau. When Esau left for the open country to hunt game and bring it back, Rebekah said to her son Jacob, "Look, I overheard your father say to your brother Esau, 'Bring me some game and prepare me some tasty food to eat, so that I may give you my blessing in the presence of the LORD before I die.' Now, my son, listen carefully and do what I tell you: Go out to the flock and bring me two choice young goats, so I can prepare some tasty food for your father, just the way he likes it. Then take it to your father to eat, so that he may give you his blessing before he dies."*
>
> *Jacob said to Rebekah his mother, "But my brother Esau is a hairy man, and I'm a man with smooth skin. What if my father touches me? I would appear to be tricking him and would bring down a curse on myself rather than a blessing."*
>
> *His mother said to him, "My son, let the curse fall on me. Just do what I say; go and get them for me." . . .*
>
> *Esau held a grudge against Jacob because of the blessing his father had given him. He said to himself, "The days of mourning for my father are near; then I will kill my brother Jacob."*
>
> *When Rebekah was told what her older son Esau had said, she sent for her younger son Jacob and said to him, "Your brother Esau is consoling himself with the thought of killing you. Now then, my son, do what I say: Flee at once to my brother Laban in Haran. Stay with him for a while until your brother's fury subsides. When your brother is no longer angry with you and forgets what you did to him, I'll send word for you*

to come back from there. Why should I lose both of you in one day?"
(Genesis 27:5-13, 41-45)

2. On a scale of 1 to 100 (100 being perfect), how well do you think
   Rebekah did in each of the following areas? Explain.
   a. making her home a safe place
   b. being involved in her children's lives without "smothering"
   c. letting natural consequences teach her children
   d. doing the right thing when her children messed up

   Now I am ready to visit you for the third time, and I will not be
   a burden to you, because what I want is not your possessions but you.
   After all, children should not have to save up for their parents, but par-
   ents for their children. So I will very gladly spend for you everything I
   have and expend myself as well. If I love you more, will you love me less?
   (2 Corinthians 12:14-15)

3. What does this passage imply about the cost of being a parent? How
   is this different from giving your kids everything they want? Based on
   your experience so far, would you say that "expending yourself" is
   worth it?

   And we know that in all things God works for the good of those who
   love him, who have been called according to his purpose. For those God
   foreknew he also predestined to be conformed to the likeness of his Son,
   that he might be the firstborn among many brothers. (Romans 8:28-29)

4. According to this passage, which of the following comes closest to
   God's goal for you? How do you feel about that?
   ____ making your children turn out "right"
   ____ becoming more like Christ
   ____ other _____

Applying the Principles

Here are some real-life stories[15] in which young people remember how their parents raised them. How might these ideas help you make the most of your power as a parent?

1. "My mom and I had many late-into-the-night discussions while sitting on my bed. She was not afraid to answer any of my questions, and no concern or frustration was too silly for her. She laughed with me, cried with me—she made me feel valuable by just wanting to be with me. These times laid a foundation of trust that made me want to ask about more spiritual matters."

   If you tried this with your child, what would be your goal?

   How might you change this activity to make it more enjoyable for you and your child?

2. "Before I got my driver's license, Daddy used to drive me about 10 minutes to school every morning. During this time we would listen to Chuck Colson's *Breakpoint* commentary on the radio and then discuss the day's topic/issue. These times helped me begin to understand the importance of having a Christian worldview, and I saw my daddy's passion for God's truth and how that relates to our culture."

   If you tried this with your child, what would be your goal?

   How might you change this activity to make it more enjoyable for you and your child?

3. "My dad and I would read Scripture, usually Proverbs, before I went to school in junior high. This kept me floating during a period when I was lukewarm in my Christian life."

If you tried this with your child, what would be your goal?

How might you change this activity to make it more enjoyable for you and your child?

4. "During high school, Dad and I would often eat breakfast together at our kitchen table, and we'd sometimes talk about spiritual questions I had. My favorite part, which encouraged me most, was when we ended that time in prayer. It really prepared me for the day."

If you tried this with your child, what would be your goal?

How might you change this activity to make it more enjoyable for you and your child?

5. "My mom did not like to cook much, but when she did I would go in the kitchen with her and talk. We would share so much about our lives, talking very openly and relating as friends. This didn't occur until I was going through adolescence and I was able to appreciate all she had given to me and to accept her unconditionally. Now she is my best friend."

If you tried this with your child, what would be your goal?

How might you change this activity to make it more enjoyable for you and your child?

Insight for Your Week

What about parents who've watched their kids "choose stupid," who've been dragged down the most dangerous detours, who've agonized and cried and prayed and made seemingly impossible choices—yet somehow survived?

Here are some of their hard-won observations.

1. *You can't control your child's choices.* Once your daughter leaves the house, there's no telling what she's doing. She can take drugs, cheat on tests, drive drunk—or study hard and land in the top 10 percent of her class. And there's nothing you can do about it.

2. *God allows all of us to make poor decisions.* Generally speaking, God doesn't step in to rescue us when we pick the wrong path. If we choose to blow through a stop sign because we're in a hurry, He doesn't stamp His foot on the brake.

3. *Allow your child to face the consequences of his choices.* One parent said, "It's really difficult to know when to step in and when to allow God to let life teach the lessons." But if God feels it's important for us to learn through the consequences of our choices, why are we shielding our kids from the consequences of theirs?

4. *Learn the art of relinquishment.* This means letting go. It may mean releasing your dream for who your child would be, giving up control, leaving the results to God.

5. *Get help for yourself and your family.* Some folks prefer pastoral counseling; others opt for a therapist. Just be sure the advice is well-founded in Scripture and in a knowledge of kids.

6. *If necessary, get your troubled child out of the house to protect the rest of the family.* When a young person becomes violent or brings home illegal activities like drug-dealing, it's time to act on behalf of your family's safety. For help in locating a program or residential facility

that might suit your situation, talk with a Christian therapist in your area—or call the counseling department at Focus on the Family (1-800-A-FAMILY).

7. *Don't be afraid to let others know what you're dealing with.* One parent admitted, "We didn't want the whole world knowing [about our prodigal teen] because my husband was an elder in the church." Many parents have been surprised at how God used their transparency to help families in similar situations.

8. *Ask for prayer.* Tell those you trust that your child is making poor choices with her life, and you'd love for them to pray. Find one or two to be prayer partners and ask them to pray for you daily.

9. *Pray.* Give Him a chance to speak to your heart, too. If you have other children, pray as a family.

10. *Don't look for good, look for God.* Some well-meaning people say, "Look for good in the situation." But sometimes there's no earthly good to be seen; sometimes there is only God. Trust that God has not abandoned you even if you don't sense His presence.

11. *Praise God.* I'm not going to tell you to thank God for your child's wandering. Instead, praise Him not *for* the chaos but in the *middle* of it— for the same reasons you've always praised Him.

12. *Take care of the rest of your family.* The child in crisis usually gets the attention. Make sure that your marriage (if you're married) and your other kids (if you have some) aren't ignored.

13. *Allow yourself some enjoyment.* Many couples who have prodigals put themselves in suspended animation, grimly hanging on "until this thing is resolved." But you can't keep going without recharging.

14. *Hold on to your core values.* Don't let the continuing attack wear you down. Did you believe before that God knows your situation, right down to the number of hairs on your head? He still does.

15. *Try writing in a journal.* Recording your thoughts, feelings, and prayers can help you sort through the garbage and discover what's important. You can use a notebook, a blank book, or a computer.

16. *Be relentless.* It's never giving up. It's moving forward no matter what. It's trying new things when old things aren't working.

17. *Be tough and tender.* That's especially true when it comes to dealing with the comments of others. Even well-meaning people can be hurtful. Don't let their barbs penetrate, but be tender enough to hear the supportive words others may offer.

18. *Don't try to play God.* You can't be the Holy Spirit. You can only be a parent who's relentlessly loving—and who leaves the results in God's hands.

—Joe White with Lissa Halls Johnson[16]

NOTES

1. Adapted from Tim Sanford, *Losing Control and Liking It* (Carol Stream, Ill.: Focus on the Family/Tyndale House Publishers, 2009), pp. 172-173.
2. Ibid., pp. 105-107, 118-120.
3. Adapted from Paul C. Reisser, M.D., et al., *Baby & Child Care* (Carol Stream, Ill.: Focus on the Family/Tyndale House Publishers, 2007), pp. 371-372.
4. Ibid., pp. 520-528.
5. Ibid., p. 469.
6. Based on Joe White, *What Kids Wish Parents Knew About Parenting* (Sisters, Ore.; Questar, 1988), pp. 176-178.
7. Adapted from Paul C. Reisser, M.D., et al., *Baby & Child Care,* pp. 401-405.
8. Ibid., p. 368.
9. Adapted from Bob Waliszewski and Bob Smithouser, et al., *Parents' Guide to the Spiritual Mentoring of Teens* (Focus on the Family/ Tyndale, 2001), pp. 339-354.
10. Adapted from Andy Braner, et al., *Parents' Guide to the Spiritual Mentoring of Teens,* pp. 317-319.
11. Ibid., pp. 319-327.
12. Adapted from Jim Weidmann, et al., *Parents' Guide to the Spiritual Mentoring of Teens,* pp. 303-304.
13. Adapted from Paul C. Reisser, M.D., et al., *Baby & Child Care,* pp. 460-461.
14. Adapted from Dr. Kevin Leman, *Home Court Advantage* (Wheaton, Ill.: Focus on the Family/Tyndale House Publishers, 2005), pp. 17-18.
15. Adapted from *Parents' Guide to the Spiritual Mentoring of Teens,* pp. 231-454.

16. Adapted from Joe White with Lissa Halls Johnson, *Sticking with Your Teen* (Carol Stream, Ill.: Focus on the Family/Tyndale House Publishers, 2006), pp. 105-115.

About Our DVD Presenters
Essentials of Parenting: Be Prepared

Dr. Archibald Hart is well known for his ministry to churches through psychological training, education, and consultation. A former dean of the School of Psychology at Fuller Theological Seminary, he is now retired from full-time teaching but continues to examine issues of stress, depression, and anxiety. Dr. Hart is the author of 24 books, including *Sleep, It Does a Family Good*; *Stressed or Depressed*; and *Safe Haven Marriage*. He and his wife, Kathleen, live in California. They have three daughters and seven grandchildren.

Dr. Julianna Slattery is a family psychologist and broadcast host for Focus on the Family. Juli is the author of *Finding the Hero in Your Husband*, *Guilt-Free Motherhood*, and *Beyond the Masquerade*. Juli earned a doctor of psychology and master of science in clinical psychology at Florida Institute of Technology, a master of arts in psychology from Biola University, and a bachelor of arts from Wheaton College. Juli and her husband, Mike, live in Colorado Springs and are the parents of three boys.

Dr. Bob Barnes is president of Sheridan House Family Ministries in Fort Lauderdale, Florida. He presents seminars and conferences on parenting and marriage throughout North America, hosts a weekly radio program, and is the author of several books for families—including *Ready for Responsibility: How to Equip Your Children for Work and Marriage* and *Raising Confident Kids*. Bob has been married to Rosemary Johnson Barnes since 1972. They have two children, Torrey and Robey.

Dannah Gresh is a best-selling author of teen and tween books—including *And the Bride Wore White* as well as *Six Ways to Keep The Little in Your Girl: Guiding Your Daughter from Her Tweens to Her Teens*. Dannah has long been at the forefront of the movement to encourage tweens and teens to be modest and to pursue purity. She is also the creator of Secret Keeper Girl, a live tour. She lives in Pennsylvania with her husband, Bob, and their teenagers, Rob, Lexi, and Autumn.

Dena Cabrera, Psy.D. is a licensed psychologist in the state of Arizona and has been on staff at Remuda Ranch Treatment Centers for 10 years. She is an expert in the assessment and treatment of eating disorders. She speaks to national audiences on state-of-the-art treatments of eating disorders and difficult mental health problems. Dr. Cabrera has written numerous articles in journals and magazines including *Christian Counseling Today*, and has co-authored chapters in *Eating Disorders: A Handbook of Christian Treatment*.

Glenn Williams is former chief operating officer of Focus on the Family. A psychologist and former pastor, he founded Focus on the Family Australia and headed the organization for 10 years. He wrote *Talking Smack: Who's Talking to Your Kids about Drugs and Alcohol, if You're Not?* and co-wrote the parenting curriculum *How To Drug Proof Your Kids*, which has been used in 11 countries. Glenn and his wife, Natalie, have three children.

Dr. Del Tackett is former president of Focus on the Family Institute and former senior vice-president of Focus on the Family. He is also the architect and chief spokesperson for Focus on the Family's The Truth Project®, a nationwide initiative designed to bring the Christian worldview to the body of Christ. He and his wife live in Colorado Springs, Colorado.

Jerusha Clark is the author or co-author of ten books, including *Every Thought Captive: Battling the Toxic Beliefs that Separate Us from the Life We Crave* and *Inside a Cutter's Mind: Understanding and Helping Those Who Self-Injure*. She and her husband, Jeramy, have two daughters.

Rebecca Hagelin has for some 25 years educated parents and civic organizations on how to understand the media culture and its affect on families. She is the president and CEO of Rebecca Hagelin Communications and Marketing, LLC. Her weekly column, "How To Save Your Family," appears in *The Washington Times*. She is the author of *Home Invasion: Protecting Your Family in a Culture That's Gone Stark Raving Mad* and *30 Ways in 30 Days to Save Your Family*. Rebecca and her husband, Andy, have two sons and a daughter.

Ron Luce is president and founder of Teen Mania Ministries, a Christian organization that reaches millions of young people worldwide. After Ron received a bachelor's degree in theology and psychology and a master's degree in counseling, he and his wife, Katie, started Teen Mania in 1986. Ron rallies teens all over the U.S. in arenas and stadiums at events called Acquire the Fire, with over 3 million attendees to date. He has written 30 books for teenagers and their parents, including *ReCreate: Building a Culture in Your Home Stronger than the Culture Deceiving Your Kids*. Ron and Katie have two daughters and a son.

Michelle Anthony, Ed.D. is pastor of family ministries at ROCKHARBOR Church in Costa Mesa, California. A former professor at Biola University and Talbot School of Theology, she is the author of *Spiritual Parenting*. She and her husband, Michael, have two children.

Daniel Huerta is a bicultural and bilingual licensed clinical social worker. He and his wife, Heather, have two children. A therapist specializing in areas affecting children, adolescents, and young adults, he also provides counseling services for Focus on the Family.

FOCUS ON THE FAMILY®

Welcome to the Family

Whether you purchased this book, borrowed it or received it as a gift, we're glad you're reading it. It's just one of the many helpful, encouraging and biblically based resources produced by Focus on the Family® for people in all stages of life.

Focus began in 1977 with the vision of one man, Dr. James Dobson, a licensed psychologist and author of numerous best-selling books on marriage, parenting and family. Alarmed by the societal, political and economic pressures that were threatening the existence of the American family, Dr. Dobson founded Focus on the Family with one employee and a once-a-week radio broadcast aired on 36 stations.

Now an international organization reaching millions of people daily, Focus on the Family is dedicated to preserving values and strengthening and encouraging families through the life-changing message of Jesus Christ.

Focus on the Family
MAGAZINES

These faith-building, character-developing publications address the interests, issues, concerns, and challenges faced by every member of your family from preschool through the senior years.

For More
INFORMATION

 ONLINE:
Log on to
FocusOnTheFamily.com
In Canada, log on to
FocusOnTheFamily.ca

 PHONE:
Call toll-free:
**800-A-FAMILY
(232-6459)**
In Canada, call toll-free:
800-661-9800

| **THRIVING FAMILY™**
Marriage & Parenting | **FOCUS ON**
THE FAMILY
CLUBHOUSE JR.®
Ages 4 to 8 | **FOCUS ON**
THE FAMILY
CLUBHOUSE®
Ages 8 to 12 | **FOCUS ON**
THE FAMILY
CITIZEN®
U.S. news issues | Rev. 4/10 |